BAKING WITH THE
ST. PAUL BREAD CLUB

Minnesota
Historical Society
Press

BAKING WITH THE ST. PAUL BREAD CLUB

RECIPES, TIPS & STORIES

KIM ODE

Recipe permissions are listed on p. 156.

www.mhspress.org

The Minnesota Historical Society Press is a member of the Association of American University Presses.

Manufactured in Canada by Friesens, Altona, Manitoba.

Baking with the St. Paul Bread Club was designed and set in type by Cathy Spengler, Minneapolis. The text type is Miller, designed by Matthew Carter. The display type is Chase, designed by Rian Hughes.

10 9 8 7 6 5 4 3 2 1

♾ The paper used in this publication meets the minimum requirements of the American National Standard for Information Sciences—Permanence for Printed Library Materials, ANSI Z39.48–1984.

International Standard Book Numbers
   ISBN 13: 978-0-87351-567-2 (cloth)
   ISBN 10: 0-87351-567-6 (cloth)

Library of Congress Cataloging-in-Publication Data
Ode, Kim, 1955–
Baking with the St. Paul Bread Club: recipes, tips, and stories / Kim Ode.
     p. cm.
Includes index.
ISBN-13: 978-0-87351-567-2 (cloth : alk. paper)
ISBN-10: 0-87351-567-6 (cloth : alk. paper)
   1. Bread. I. Title.

TX769.O34 2006
641.8'15—dc22

2006012638

For John, who lights all my fires

CONTENTS

ACKNOWLEDGMENTS

This book came to life because of the work, insights, and support of many people. My thanks first go to all the members of the St. Paul Bread Club for keeping alive the tradition of home-baked bread and most especially to those who opened their kitchens, hearts, and recipe files for this book. Thanks also to Klecko, the human incarnation of bread's symbolic generosity, for opening his world to me, and to Larry Burns and Gary Sande, the owners of the St. Agnes Baking Company, for making the delightfully uncorporate decision to open their bakery's doors to us. I'm grateful to my calming editor, Pam McClanahan, who had the idea and vision for this project and opened my eyes to the possibilities of a book. Immeasurable love and gratitude go to my mom, who inspires me by always being open to new and different recipes, and to my father, who always tries everything with an open mind. My deepest thanks go to John, Austin, and Mimi for their patience and support and their open hearts, and open mouths, whenever I take yet another loaf of bread from the oven and call it dinner.

INTRODUCTION

It wasn't until a few years ago, after I had started baking bread for my family with a convert's intensity, that I began to appreciate the sacrifice my mother had made each time she shook loose a loaf of bread from a hot pan.

Her fresh bread never took me by surprise. All morning the big yellow Pyrex bowl would sit on the counter, the drape of the dish towel subtly shifting as the dough swelled past the rim. By afternoon the bread was in pans, the kitchen filling with the metallic whiff of a preheating oven.

The beauty of this incremental process was how it let me arrange my day. I could bike along the road leading to and from our farm, then swing for an hour on the bag of straw hanging on a rope from the hayloft's rafters, and then pet the new kittens—there were always new kittens—timing each diversion so that I could walk into the kitchen just when Mom was tapping the loaves to hear if they sounded hollow. Even when they were still too hot to handle, still too tender to cut, she would slice the end off of one and pass it to me.

There is nothing like a slice of hot, fresh bread, the steam still rising through a sheen of butter. Especially the heel of a loaf, she'd say, and with a child's breathtaking selfishness, I would agree and eat the whole thing.

Today, in my own kitchen, I also let that first hot slice go to the child—or the husband—who just happens to be thirsty or checking the thermostat or riffling through the junk drawer looking for a whatchamajig as I'm easing a loaf from the oven. I could claim that slice for my own. But I hand it over, even while imagining the faint resistance of the crust and give of the crumb between my own teeth. And it's OK, because I know that others have arranged their day around bread.

That may even be the whole point.

We talk a lot about the desire for community these days. We wonder at how the Internet enables people to connect over a mind-boggling array of passions. We live in amazing times. But I'm throwing in my lot with those who marvel over the connection we can make over a loaf of home-baked bread.

Several years ago, Dan "Klecko" McGleno founded the St. Paul Bread Club, a loose affiliation of home bakers from around the Twin Cities. Four times a year, Klecko opens the doors of the St. Agnes Baking Company, just north of downtown St. Paul and not far from where the city's first gristmill was built on Phalen Creek in 1842. He's production manager there and saw the club as a way to give bakers of varying experience the chance to talk bread, trade tips, hear what a master baker advises, bake their own dough, and eat each others' bread.

It's a community that almost slipped from our grasp.

Well, that may be a bit of an exaggeration, the sort of modern navel-gazing that lets us imagine our homely lives as pivot points in time. The fact is that people have been baking bread for ten thousand years without pause. We've always gathered over bread. In 1849, when the city of St. Paul issued its first business directory, there were five bakers—more than the tally of doctors, shoemakers, gunsmiths, wheelwrights, blacksmiths, or harness makers.

But over time we've baked less. As with beating our clothes on river rocks or plucking the feathers from our chickens, the ability to pay someone else to do our household chores was a sign of our progress. Likewise, the ability to lay a platter of bread as white as Elmer's Glue on our dinner table showed our success: We could afford to buy bread made with flour carefully and expensively sifted free of its whole grain origins.

It's funny now to think of something as modest as Wonder Bread as a symbol of domestic progress. But it's sobering to realize how gradual changes in bread can define a generation. Several of the home bakers in this book recalled how their kids groaned at the prospect of school lunch sandwiches made with Mom's cracked wheat bread. None of the other kids' lunches looked like something that came from a log cabin—maybe even a cave. Or so it felt.

At our house there's still always a loaf of airy, store-bought English muffin bread for my son's peanut butter and jelly sandwiches—and even that's a little on the sturdy side for grilled cheese sandwiches, as far as my daughter is concerned. They like my crackly baguettes, pizza-friendly *focaccias*, or chewy *ciabattas*. But anything sourdough is the object of painstaking courtesy; they don't want to hurt my feelings, but well, it's not really their favorite.

So I choose my battles and give thanks that our household never entertained the low-carb revolution, a stance I regard as a victory of common sense and moderation. More and more, people are coming back to bread, finding the truth in the old punch line about the downside of a longer life: It just means more years of denial. Barely three years ago, close to 10 percent of U.S. adults were on the Atkins Diet; in 2005 the Atkins Nutritional Company filed for bankruptcy after that proportion fell to 2 percent.

At the same time the act of baking bread has changed more in the past twenty-five years than it has in the past five hundred. The invention of the bread machine alone has inspired legions of people to delve into the world of yeast, not to mention solving the "office gift" dilemma for many weddings.

Cookbook sales are growing and the number of books devoted solely to bread continues to climb. So we have rediscovered bread. Now we need to rediscover our skills and, through them, a community of home bakers. It sounds like a pretty straightforward goal, yet it's not as simple as I once thought.

A story: Back in 2001 I was thumbing through the course catalog for the North House Folk School in Grand Marais, Minnesota. The school teaches traditional northern crafts and champions the philosophy of the Scandinavian *folkehøjskole,* where learning is valued for its own sake.

I was a columnist for the *Star Tribune* and mired in one of my occasional funks about the transience of daily newspapering. So when I saw a class on how to build a wood-fired brick bread oven, I knew that's what I had to do. Here was something that would last the ages. And I was determined to do it all by myself.

I had no idea what I was getting into, only sure that my labors would have a tangible result, from which tangible rewards would follow. I'd always loved bread and had always meant to get more serious about making it. So I signed up and, with a dozen others, learned from master oven-builder Alan Scott the mysteries of mortar, load-bearing archways, airflow, and precise measurements.

I returned home to find that what I really needed was my dozen classmates, but I stubbornly kept everyone at bay. The project took months, from finding the materials to hauling them to our backyard—about three thousand pounds of stuff, all told—to transforming them into an oven. I had to stop work for the winter when temperatures dropped too low for the mortar to cure. I finally accepted my husband's offer of help, and he built the framing over which he then flung stucco. (This also is why he gets those first slices of hot bread.)

Friends were skeptical of my venture, to say the least. But I assured them that I had a goal much larger than simply building an outdoor oven.

One evening, I was regaling a friend about this grander plan, telling her how I wanted to re-create the culture of a French village where neighbors would bring their risen dough to the communal oven. As our breads emerged, our bonds would strengthen. Gathered at the hearth, friends and neighbors would build connections that would cross the boundaries of gender, age, politics, and class. Finally, I noticed the half-quizzical, half-pitying look on her face.

"But Ode," she said, "you're the only one I know who bakes bread!"

Hmmm. I had to admit that she was right. The community of home bakers is not exactly invading the ranks of American life like aproned soldiers pouring from some Trojan horse. Yet after decades of baking less, we are beginning to bake more. It's a start. I credit the renaissance of artisanal breads for reawakening us to the satisfaction available in a bite of sourdough flecked with wild rice or a rye bread born of a long rise. Far from discouraging us from trying our hand, I think the growing number of terrific bakeries are inspiring us to give baking a try.

Over and over, the bakers in this book volunteered how making bread is a sort of therapy. For those who favor sourdough, there is the ritual of feeding the starter, a regular nurturing of something that is as alive as any other member of their family. Don't smirk. In fact, bakers often name their sourdough starters in a nod to what's become one of the more reliable relationships in their lives. Even bakers who've long resisted names as a corny conceit end up relenting. And so my bubbly starter eventually was christened "Glinda," after the good witch in *The Wizard of Oz.*

Kneading, however, is where most of the therapy lies. If there were a study assessing the mental health of people who, on a regular basis, kneaded a shaggy boulder of dough into a bouncy, satiny orb, I'm convinced that they would set a new high standard for even-keeledness.

A session of kneading compels us to be alone with our thoughts, a condition that seems increasingly endangered, as a glance down any store aisle or at the next lane of traffic will tell you. Simply put, you cannot knead bread while talking on a cell phone.

Kneading is a full-body experience, a leaning in and pushing through all the way from your firmly planted feet to your shifting shoulders. A really stiff dough should leave you a little winded. As it grows smoother and bouncier, the dough absorbs frustrations about a job, worries about a parent, anxieties about a teen, and even last night's argument. Why bore your friends? Your dough will not only absorb these things but transform itself into comfort food.

This is where you come in.

This book is for the growing community of bakers, from the experienced to the novice. In it members of the St. Paul Bread Club have shared not so much how they bake but why they bake. After all, the how is not really such a secret, having been shared since Egypt's earliest history. But the why can be a revelation, whether it's a means of monitoring healthy ingredients, of honoring an ethnic culture, or of seeking some respite in a busy life. Best of all, these bakers believe in the power of a shared recipe.

So here is a baker's dozen of club members who have shared some of their favorite recipes, tips, and epiphanies, whether they have baked for several years or several decades. There is advice for the beginning baker, standards for measurement and methods, and random crumbs of baking wisdom from people over the centuries.

The seventy recipes within range from a straightforward white sandwich loaf to a rather elaborate Slovenian *potica,* and I have either tested each recipe or watched as the baker mixed and kneaded. Many of the breads are distinctive riffs on whole grains, variously shaped, sweetened or studded with that baker's preferred ingredients. There are two challahs, but they're quite different and, indeed, invite you to give them your own interpretation. There are two Swedish rye breads, but they're mere cousins, like the old fable of the simple country mouse and the snazzy city mouse.

Many breads have an ethnic vibe, with favorite recipes from Germany, Sweden, Switzerland, India, Ireland, and Italy. But there are also some classics: cinnamon rolls, muffins, and cloverleaf buns. Bread is born for embellishing, so we have jalapeño breadsticks, a Cheddar cheese loaf, and a recipe that may have you scavenging your bird feeder. Here are recipes for the sumptuous black bread served at the Saint Paul Hotel and the herb-flecked bread from St. Paul's Ristorante Luci. There's the wild rice sourdough once served to former Soviet president Mikhail Gorbachev.

Sourdough breads are more involved than basic yeast breads, but they are an integral part of this book, thanks to Klecko's influence. He's been nurturing his unusual brick starter for eighteen years and has generously shared his formula. You'll have to plan ahead to make the sourdough loaves, allowing a week to ten days to build your starter. But each batch will get better over the years as your brick develops its own personality. You will find yourself giving it a name. Don't hurry. It will come to you.

In addition, there's practical information for the beginning bread baker and insider tips for the more experienced. There are guidelines for starting your own bread club, a discussion of favorite ingredients, and within each chapter a list of the profiled baker's most well-worn cookbooks.

The recipes follow the story of each baker, so you can get a sense of who they are and then an appreciation of what they bake. There's also an index to more easily find specific breads. Eventually, the dog-eared pages will help you find your favorites.

These days, baking no longer is a chore but a choice. The home bakers profiled here would like to help. Their intent is little different from the purpose noted in a 1916 pamphlet distributed by the Ramsey County Flour Company, makers of Miss Saint Paul Flour. In it baking expert P. O. Walker opened on this confident note: "In placing this booklet in your hands we feel that we are positively benefiting you, your family and your community."

Cooking, he added, relies on two essential skills: knowing how and using good judgment. "These two things go far towards making house work either a task or a pleasure. To some it is drudgery, to others it is an accomplishment," he wrote. "And here let me say, many people would rather eat your good rolls or bread than they would hear your good music."

I'm pretty sure he meant that to sound inspiring. So let's bake.

BREAD WISDOM

(FOR BEGINNERS & OTHERS)

When I talk to people about baking bread, they often respond in one of two ways. Either they're intimidated by the process, talking of this mysterious "knack" that they believe one must possess, or they sputter that they don't have the time.

The issue of not having the time will disappear as you read how these bakers have learned how a day can easily be structured around bread. But here are some terms you'll run across in the course of this book that may need some clarification and will go a long way toward acquiring the knack.

Hey, I'm telling you all of our secrets. Pay attention.

Terms

Baguette (ba-GET). This long, thin loaf with a crispy crust and an open crumb (see *crumb*) is often referred to as "French bread," though French bread is not necessarily baguette. Imagine them poking out of a cycling youth's backpack as he darts home through the streets of Paris.

Baking stone or tiles. Often called a "pizza stone," this widely available tool gives your homemade pizzas a crispier crust. It's important to preheat a stone at least thirty minutes before baking. Also, be careful if adding water to your oven for steam as stones or tiles can crack, which doesn't make them unusable, just less convenient.

Batard (ba-TARD). This torpedo-shaped loaf is formed by patting the dough into a rectangle, folding the sides toward each other in thirds—like folding a business letter—and then rolling it into a cylinder, the ends tapering to a gentle point. The dough can either stay this shape or, after being allowed to rest briefly, be rolled into longer baguettes.

Bench knife. A stainless steel, multipurpose baker's tool, about 3-by-6-inches, with a sharp edge that enables you to easily divide dough, to scoop and fold an especially sticky dough until it firms up, or to scrape clean your work surface. Once you own a bench knife, you will want to scratch your name into it.

Boule (bool). This round loaf is rolled firmly upon itself into a ball and then pinched tightly together on the bottom to create a surface tension. This helps the dough keep its shape instead of spreading as it proofs.

Bread flour versus all-purpose flour. Flour is differentiated by the amount of gluten, or protein, it contains. All-purpose flour, ground mostly from soft wheat, has less gluten than bread flour, which is ground from hard red winter wheat. Think of gluten as the culinary equivalent of a toned athlete's "six-pack abs": It's the elastic network that gives a hunk of dough the strength to rise and expand and hold in the yeasty gas without breaking down or collapsing. Some breads need that muscle to support their lofty, chewy interiors. Other breads, notably quick breads, are better with the slightly paunchier nature of all-purpose flour. In any case, use unbleached flour; it's less processed and lends bread a creamier color.

Butter. Most bakers use unsalted butter, also called sweet butter, to guard against a too-salty result. The idea is that it keeps the salt content to the amount you add as seasoning. Plus, unsalted butter usually is made from higher-grade butter. But if you get the urge to bake and all you have on hand is regular butter, use it and be a little stingy with the recipe's salt. The world won't end.

Crumb. This term refers to the texture of the finished loaf. Breads with small, closely spaced holes are said to have a "fine crumb," whereas breads with large, irregular holes are said to have an "open crumb." For example, a delicate challah or dense rye has a fine crumb, while a baguette or foccacia riddled with airy holes has an open crumb.

Flours. A number of different flours and grains are mentioned in this book: bulgur, millet, polenta, graham, semolina. Most large grocery stores stock these, but local food co-ops are the home bread baker's friend. Many of these whole-grain ingredients are best stored in the freezer, especially if you buy them in large quantities or bake only occasionally, because the oils in the germ and bran can go rancid over time. And another note: flours do not need to be sifted when used in breads.

Lukewarm. This term seems fraught with subjectivity, but it's not that complicated. The important thing to know is that you should err on the side of too cool rather than too warm to keep from accidentally killing your yeast in hot water. Basically, this means a temperature in which you can easily hold your finger. If you have an instant-read thermometer, lukewarm is 110° F or lower. In baking, as in life, it's better to be too cool than too hot.

Malt syrup. Also known as barley malt syrup, this sweetener is available in more grocery stores these days and also in local co-ops. It contributes a depth to a loaf's color and flavor.

Peel. This wooden paddle is often seen working pies in and out of ovens at artisanal pizza places and is also readily available at most any department store. Sprinkle its smooth surface with cornmeal, and your bread will easily slide off onto the baking stone that's been preheating in your oven.

Poolish. This mixture, while similar to sponge, often uses less yeast for an even slower rise. See also *sponge*.

Pullman loaf pan. This long rectangular pan has a sliding, tight-fitting lid that results in a loaf that is almost a perfect block with a thin crust all around. It can be found in specialty kitchen stores or from online vendors.

Punch down. After a dough's first rise, you need to gently deflate the mass, either to form the loaves or to allow for a second rise. The term "punch" is perhaps too aggressive a description of the necessary action. And yet, standing before a quavering pillow of dough, the impulse often is irresistible.

Rise until doubled. Most breads have two rises, the first after the dough has been mixed and another after it's been shaped prior to baking. The second rise is also known as *proofing*. During each rise the fermentation creates carbon dioxide in the dough, causing it to swell. If the dough is allowed to swell to more than double its original size, it may collapse, so you will want to know when it has just doubled its size. Overproofing is a bigger problem during the second rise because your yeast, quite literally, is about out of gas. Some bakers recommend using the same bowl or pan each time so that you can familiarize yourself with what your dough looks like at each stage.

Salt. Various recipes call for different salts. Table salt is the default choice, but many bakers prefer kosher or sea salt because it is not iodized. Kosher salt comes in larger flakes and so measures differently; a measuring spoon should be slightly mounded when using kosher salt. As with most culinary adventures, err on the side of less salt when first mixing because you can always add more, but can never take it away. The big-grained *fleur de sel*, available in gourmet stores, is for sprinkling on top of a bread, such as foccacia.

Scoring. This pattern of slashes across the top of a loaf is made with a sharp knife, scissors, or a razor blade. The scores release steam as the bread bakes, which both helps keep a loaf from exploding crazily from one side and enhances its appearance.

Shaping. Forming dough into rounds, baguettes, loaves, or buns mostly is a matter of creating tension. Not in you; in the dough. A well-shaped loaf has a springy taut appearance without being overly tight. A too-tight loaf may split as it proofs or bakes. And use little or no flour when you shape; friction between a tacky dough and a clean surface is what makes a smooth shape.

For rounds, fold the dough in half, tucking the ends toward the bottom and pinching them together to create a surface tension. Then firmly cradle the dough with your hands and turn in small circular motions on an un-floured countertop. The friction will cause the seam to seal and the surface to stretch into a smooth sphere. The same technique can be used to form buns: cup one hand over the dough and turn in small circles on the countertop to create the needed friction.

For baguettes, pat the dough into a rectangle, then fold the long ends toward the middle, as you might for a business letter, then press a crease down the center and bring up the sides, pinching them together to form a surface tension. Roll it to the desired length and place seam side down on a baking sheet.

For dough to be placed in loaf pans, pat the dough into a rectangle, then fold the long ends toward the middle, as for a business letter, then press a crease down the center and pinch together the sides to form a surface tension. Place seam side down in the pan.

Sounds hollow. When a loaf of bread is done baking, it makes a hollow sound if thumped on the bottom, meaning that there's no longer any dense, unbaked dough in the middle. Knowing the correct sound is one of those things that comes with experience. To hear the difference, remove a loaf from the oven about fifteen minutes before it's supposed to be done and thump the bottom; return it to the oven until the buzzer goes off and thump it again. It should sound different—hollower.

Sourdough starter. This mixture of flour and water absorbs wild yeasts from the air to create a natural leavening agent. Starters can include other ingredients such as potatoes or grapes and also are made with different flours. Fed regularly, they can last for centuries. They are used instead of yeast but also can be supplemented with yeast.

Sponge. This premix comprises flour, water, and yeast and ferments several hours or overnight, helping to boost the flavor of your bread.

Tempering. This technique is for combining beaten eggs with a hot mixture without "cooking" the eggs before they are incorporated. To do this, whisk a small amount of the hot mixture into the bowl of beaten eggs to warm them, then whisk the warmed eggs back into the bowl of hot mixture.

Vital wheat gluten. This is the natural protein found in wheat. A small amount added to yeast bread recipes improves the texture and elasticity of the dough. It can be found in the flour section of supermarkets.

Yeast. Almost every recipe here calls for active dry yeast. Each also calls for proofing the yeast to make sure that it's active. Yeast is of such quality these days that it's rare to find "dead" yeast unless it's been languishing on your shelves or the back of your refrigerator. But it never hurts to test it. A timesaver, though, is the instant or quick-rise yeast often marketed as bread machine yeast. It's finer-grained and can be stirred into the flour without first needing to be activated by liquid. Because it's finer, it measures out slightly less than the amount of regular yeast called for. But the two varieties really can be used interchangeably; don't sweat it.

The Two Most Important Techniques

Measure

Measuring flour correctly is the key to making a successful dough and keeping it from becoming dense or dry. Add it sparingly, especially while kneading. Flour is best measured with a scale. One cup of flour generally weighs between four and four and a half ounces. But dry measuring cups are fine as long as you spoon the flour in without packing it or shaking it down. Mound the flour in the cup, and then level it with a knife.

One basic rule of measuring: Your classic nested measuring cups are designed for dry ingredients, while your old Pyrex measuring cup is for wet ingredients. The difference is subtle, but exists. For bread bakers, however, heeding how a dough feels as it's being mixed and kneaded will help you determine if you need a bit more flour or a bit more water—especially since environmental conditions of your kitchen often play a role.

Knead

Kneading is what many bakers refer to as the therapeutic or meditative part of baking. Kneading isn't meant to be gentle, but to develop the flour's gluten, which gives bread its shape and flavor. You really have to have some dough in front of you to "get" kneading, but it's nothing more than firmly pushing the dough away from you, folding it over on itself, turning it ninety degrees, and then repeating the process. Push, fold, turn. Repeat until the dough becomes springy and smooth. Some recommend slapping the dough hard on the counter (make sure you don't have too much flour spread; this is why bakers wear white). Others use a more stretching motion. The point is to exercise the dough. The cool thing is that you can feel its texture change beneath your palms.

Any flat surface works for kneading, but it will feel better if it's about as low as your hands hanging at your side—which pretty much says custom built. Just go as low as possible. And try to use as little flour as possible. Patience in those first few sticky minutes will be rewarded as the dough firms up.

Gear

You don't need much to bake: a big bowl, a spatula, measuring cups and spoons, plastic wrap, a dish towel, a sharp knife, and a baking sheet or a loaf pan. So what's in all those catalogs and cooking stores? More stuff. Good stuff. Fun stuff. But remember: it's extra stuff.

About Bread Machines

I've never used one, but many people swear by them. Those who love them will know how to adapt these recipes to them. But there's room for compromise. A bread machine is fast and convenient and less messy when it comes to mixing and kneading the dough and seeing it through its first rise. But some home bakers then prefer removing the risen dough from the machine and using their hands to form a final, free-form shape. This lets them vary the shapes, add toppings such as seeds or herbs, or make decorative scoring. Better crust, too. Everyone's a winner.

Serving and Storing

Don't store bread in the refrigerator. Don't store bread in the refrigerator. Don't store bread in the refrigerator. OK?

Chilling the bread will make it go stale faster. Better to keep it in a paper bag, cut side down, for the first day and then in a plastic bag—again, cut side down—for longer.

Bread freezes well if it's double wrapped in plastic wrap and then placed in a freezer bag. But use it as quickly as possible. Leave plenty of time for a loaf of bread to thaw, a day on the counter if possible. Don't be tempted to thaw it in the microwave. I have and will when I again fail to plan far enough ahead, but it's not the best.

Refresh a thawed loaf for about ten minutes in a low oven, 225° F.

And here's a tip for the bread basket: to hold in the heat of a warm loaf, line the basket with aluminum foil and then cover the foil with a cloth or a napkin that can fold around the bread.

THE BAKERS
& THEIR RECIPES

Susan Steger Welsh

WHY I BAKE BREAD

[Bread baking is] one of those almost hypnotic businesses, like a dance from some ancient ceremony. It leaves you filled with one of the world's sweetest smells. There is no chiropractic treatment, no Yoga exercise, no hour of meditation in a music-throbbing chapel that will leave you emptier of bad thoughts than this homely ceremony of making bread.

M. F. K. FISHER, *The Art of Eating*

Classrooms are great for certain pursuits. Books are essential for particular aspects of an education. But then there's the knowledge that enters our brains through our fingers, through our noses, through the instincts that live in our guts.

This is the wisdom that's passed by rubbing elbows with it. That's how Susan Steger Welsh keeps learning about bread, and pretty much everything that catches her fancy: "Find someone who knows what they're doing and hang out with them."

Hanging out is crucial to a pursuit built on such subjective terms as "enough flour for medium-soft dough," "rise until doubled," and the notorious "bake until done." Susan joined the St. Paul Bread Club to hang out with others who knew that kneading is believing. Through her involvement with the club, she's gleaned the sort of expertise that she still gets from reading her late mother's old cookbooks, studying her mother's fading notes jotted in the margins of especially dog-eared pages. In a way, she's still hanging out with her mom.

Her mother liked to read cookbooks in bed, finding them pleasurable companions with which to end the day. She was a woman ahead of her time, Susan said, a master of stir-fries and a seeker of fresh vegetables in the 1960s. "But if she ever tried yeast bread, I never heard about it. It seems like people either cook or bake."

Ah, the cooking–baking dichotomy. The observation often comes up when people talk about food. But it's less a judgment on either than an acknowledgment that passions often sort themselves between a sauté pan and an oven. For Susan the urge to follow the baker's path was linked to the pace of the task. Young and single, she worked in a deadline-driven TV newsroom. "Most of my life was happening fast. Making bread sounded slow and relaxing." And, she figured, how hard could this be?

Now fifty-two, she's learned that a more telling measure of bread— or of any pursuit, for that matter—isn't whether something is easy or hard but how much creativity it allows. "I love that spirit of trying odd things or thinking about a bread in a new way. When I look at a recipe now, I hardly ever follow it as written." Granted, this lends an element of risk to the task. "Not every loaf I make is perfect," Susan said, laughing. "My daughter will say, 'Mom, this loaf isn't very, uh, tall.'"

Most of Susan's creativity is rooted in nutrition. She's found that bread is an excellent stealth vehicle for healthy embellishments, unlike the spaghetti sauce that inevitably betrays its lacing of grated carrots. Her undercover tactics may inspire hoots of derision from the kids, but the bread always gets eaten. "I tend to try to sneak in healthful things, like canola oil for butter or some whole wheat or soy flour for white. If my family had a choice, they would have white bread with sugar every day, but I say, uh-uh, you're not getting that."

She once wrote an essay, "Why I Bake Bread," partly to answer those who wonder why people bother, especially with the growing number of artisans' bakeries. "My cupboard," she wrote, "looks like a shelf at the local co-op, stocked with bags and jars of bread flour, whole wheat flour, rye flour, oatmeal, wheat bran, oat bran, cracked wheat, soy protein, powdered milk and wheat germ. Folic acid, B vitamins, complex carbohydrates, fiber: check, check, check, check. They'll thank me some day."

Someday her kids may find themselves paging through the notebook into which she's copied her own favorite recipes. Whereas Susan's mother was ahead of her time, the daughter resists the modern idea of putting her recipes onto her computer. "I should, because the notebook is starting to fall apart, but what a job!" Besides, a computer screen doesn't show the stains that signify a well-used recipe.

The chances of her recipes ever being lost to the ages are slim, though, partly because she occasionally does lose them. Thus her strategy: "I give out my recipes to as many people who ask, so when I lose them, I can just call a friend and say, 'Hey, do you have my recipe for whatever?'" she said. "I've learned to protect myself from my shortcomings."

Her educational philosophy of hanging out came full circle a few Christmases ago when her son came home to their Macalester College neighborhood for the holidays. "He said, 'Hey Mom, teach me how to make cinnamon bread.'" So she showed him how an active yeast will make soft shoulders in a cup of water as it proofs. She taught him how to tell the temperature of lukewarm water on his wrist, how to knead a medium-soft dough, what doubled looks like, and how to thump a loaf to see if it's done.

It was a natural outcome of what she'd written in her essay on bread:

When my kids were little, I used to bring them the bowl after the dough had completed its first rise and let them punch the dough down. Their faces lit up to see the dough deflate after their little fists went into it. What power!

Back at college her son wrote home after making his first solo batch. "He said it turned out great," she said proudly but also a little wistfully. "This is what's wonderful about being nineteen years old; you don't know enough to be intimidated; you just get out there and do it."

Cracked Wheat Bread

This bread took second place in the whole wheat category in the St. Paul Bread Club's 2004 baking contest. Its slightly nubbly texture is especially striking when baked as braids. **MAKES 2 LOAVES.**

2	cups boiling water
1½	cups cracked wheat
½	cup oat bran
½	cup brown sugar or honey
2	tablespoons canola oil
1	teaspoon salt

2 packages active dry yeast
½ cup warm water
1 cup whole wheat flour
4 to 4½ cups bread flour

In a large mixing bowl combine boiling water, cracked wheat, oat bran, brown sugar or honey, oil, and salt. Let cool to lukewarm.

In a small bowl dissolve yeast in warm water; let soften. Add dissolved yeast to wheat mixture, and then beat in the wheat and bread flour, adding just enough flour to make a moderately stiff dough. Turn out onto a lightly floured surface, and knead until smooth and elastic. Place in a lightly oiled bowl, turning to coat top, cover with plastic wrap, and let rise in a warm place until doubled, about 1½ hours.

When doubled, punch down, turn out onto the counter, and shape into 2 loaves, placing each into a greased bread pan. Alternatively, for a braided loaf divide dough into 6 pieces, and roll into 12-inch ropes. Braid three ropes together to form a loaf, tucking ends under; the loaves may be baked as free-form loaves or in bread pans.

Cover with a cloth, and let rise until doubled, about 1½ hours.

Preheat oven to 400° F.

For a hard crust either spray loaves with water before placing in oven, or brush tops with an egg wash of 1 beaten egg and 1 teaspoon water and sprinkle with sesame seeds.

Bake for 30 minutes for braids; 35 to 40 minutes for loaves.

Squash Rolls

Susan adapted the recipe for these golden, subtly flavored rolls from her old Gold Medal Century of Success Cookbook: The Best Gold Medal Recipes of 100 Years. If you don't have time to bake a squash, you can use frozen squash, completely thawed and drained. This also makes great sandwich bread when baked in a loaf pan. **MAKES ABOUT 24 ROLLS OR 2 LOAVES.**

1	cup lowfat milk
2	tablespoons canola oil
½	cup sugar
1	teaspoon salt
1	package active dry yeast
¼	cup warm water
1	cup cooked winter squash, mashed
1	cup whole wheat flour
3½	to 4 cups bread flour

In a saucepan heat milk, oil, sugar, and salt just to lukewarm, stirring to dissolve sugar. In the large bowl of an electric mixer, dissolve yeast in warm water. Stir in milk mixture, squash, whole wheat flour, and 1 cup of bread flour. Beat until smooth. Gradually incorporate remaining flour until dough is easy to handle.

Turn out onto a lightly floured surface, and knead until smooth and elastic, about 5 minutes. Place in an oiled bowl, turning to coat top. Cover with plastic wrap, and let rise in a warm place until doubled, about 1½ hours. The dough is ready if a slight indentation remains when you press it.

Punch down dough, and divide and shape into 1-inch balls, placing three balls each into 24 greased muffin cups. If making loaves, divide dough in half, shape into 2 loaves, and place in greased loaf pans. Cover with a cloth, and let rise until doubled, about 45 minutes.

Preheat oven to 400° F.

Bake until light brown, about 15 to 20 minutes for rolls and 40 to 45 minutes for loaves.

Ooey Gooey Bread

Susan says the hardest part of this recipe is fending off the family for the fifteen minutes that the bread needs to cool before slicing it. Potato water makes this bread especially tender. Whenever she boils potatoes, Susan saves and refrigerates the cooking water in a sealed container until she's ready to bake. (If it will be longer than a few weeks, freeze the water.) Potato flakes work fine, too. **MAKES 3 LOAVES.**

1¾	cups potato water or 1¾ cups water mixed with 2 teaspoons instant potato flakes
1¾	cups lowfat milk
8	tablespoons (1 stick) unsalted butter
1⅓	cups honey
1	tablespoon salt
1	cup rolled oats
2	packages active dry yeast
⅔	cup bran (All-Bran cereal works, too)
6	tablespoons wheat germ
1	cup whole wheat flour
7	cups bread flour, about
½	cup white sugar
½	cup light brown sugar, packed
2	teaspoons cinnamon

Heat potato water, milk, and butter in a saucepan over low heat. As it warms, add honey and salt. When mixture comes to a boil, add rolled oats, remove from heat, and let cool to lukewarm.

Transfer to a large mixing bowl. Stir in yeast and let stand for a few minutes until softened. Add bran and wheat germ, and then beat in whole wheat and bread flour. Turn out onto a lightly floured surface, and knead until elastic and springy. The dough will be soft and sticky, but resist the urge to add too much additional flour. Turn into a lightly oiled bowl, turning to coat top, cover with plastic wrap, and let rise until doubled, about 2 hours.

Mix together white sugar, brown sugar, and cinnamon.

Turn dough out onto a lightly floured surface, and divide into 3 pieces. Roll each piece into a 12-inch-by-8-inch rectangle, and sprinkle with 4 tablespoons of sugar mixture. Take a rectangle and fold the left third to the center and the right third over that, as you'd fold a business letter. Rotate the dough 90 degrees, and roll out again into a rectangle, sprinkling with another 4 tablespoons of sugar mixture. Fold as before. Form dough into a loaf shape, and place seam side down in a greased loaf pan. Repeat with remaining 2 pieces of dough.

Cover pans with a cloth, and let rise until doubled, about 1 hour.

Preheat oven to 350° F.

Bake for 25 minutes. Remove from oven, lightly cover with aluminum foil, and bake for another 20 minutes or until loaf makes a hollow sound when removed from pan and tapped on bottom. Cool at least 15 minutes before slicing.

SUSAN'S BAKING TIPS

• An instant-read thermometer pushed to the center of most loaves (from the side to keep from marring the top) will read 190° F when they're done. (Dense sourdough or whole grain breads should reach 200 to 210° F.) I had always relied on smell and the thump-for-a-hollow-sound test. But once I began substituting ingredients and baking heartier loaves, I sometimes found that loaves that sounded done were in fact still a little gummy in the middle. The loaf of Ooey Gooey Bread is prone to this problem. But with an internal temperature reading, I can be confident that the loaf is truly done.

• Lighten up! When I first took home some of Klecko's sourdough starter, I fretted about keeping it fed. Precisely how much of what ingredi-

ent did it need to be happy? It turns out that starter is really not all that picky. I keep it in a plastic pitcher in my refrigerator, and every couple weeks I throw in a cup of bread flour, a cup of white rye flour, a cup of instant potato flakes, a cup of water, a tablespoon or so of cider vinegar, and if I happen to have it, a couple tablespoons of powdered gluten, which I get at the neighborhood co-op. I stir it up and let it sit.

• I use about a cup of starter in a two-loaf batch, along with a packet of dry yeast. I experimented with one rise versus two and found that a sourdough has a lighter texture (bigger holes, which I like) if it rises only once. If I can, I let it rise overnight in the refrigerator; the slow rise produces a more complex flavor.

High-protein Three-grain Bread

Susan says that despite its sober and virtuous name, this moist, dense loaf disappears quickly. It also makes good dinner rolls. **MAKES 2 LOAVES OR 2 DOZEN DINNER ROLLS.**

2½	cups boiling water
1	cup rolled oats
¾	cup nonfat dry milk
½	cup soy flour
¼	cup wheat germ
¼	cup brown sugar, packed
¼	cup honey
1	teaspoon salt
3	tablespoons canola oil
2	packages active dry yeast
1	teaspoon sugar
½	cup warm water
2	cups whole wheat flour
3	to 4 cups bread flour

In a large bowl combine boiling water, rolled oats, nonfat dry milk, soy flour, wheat germ, brown sugar, honey, salt, and canola oil. Mix and let cool to lukewarm. In a small bowl combine yeast, sugar, and warm water, letting it foam. Add yeast mixture to oats mixture, and then slowly mix in whole wheat and bread flour.

Turn out onto a lightly floured surface, and knead until smooth and elastic. Turn into a lightly oiled bowl, turning to coat top, cover with plastic wrap, and let rise until doubled, about 1½ hours. Punch down and form into 2 loaves, placing each into a greased loaf pan. Alternatively, make 24 dinner rolls, each about the size of a golf ball, placing them on a greased sheet pan. Cover with a cloth, and let rise until doubled, about 1 hour.

Preheat oven to 375° F.

Bake 40 minutes for loaves and 20 to 25 minutes for rolls.

Ristorante Luci's Italian Herb Bread

Ristorante Luci, a St. Paul landmark, was gracious enough to share this recipe for its trademark bread. It's great as written, but Susan likes to adapt recipes for her sourdough starter. If you keep one on hand, use a cup of starter in place of one of the packages of active dry yeast. Using sourdough starter will also let you eliminate one of this bread's three rises. **MAKES 3 LOAVES.**

2	packages active dry yeast or 1 package yeast and 1 cup sourdough starter
3	cups whole milk
1¼	cups all-purpose flour
6½	cups bread flour
2½	tablespoons sugar
1½	tablespoons salt
½	tablespoon minced garlic
1	tablespoon minced onion
1	tablespoon Italian herbs in whatever combination you prefer
½	cup olive oil

Warm milk in a saucepan or a microwave to 90 degrees or just until lukewarm. Stir in yeast, and let sit until yeast is foamy, about 5 minutes.

In a large bowl combine dry ingredients, garlic, onion, and herbs, and mix thoroughly. Drizzle in ½ cup olive oil. Slowly add milk and yeast mixture. Continue mixing until dough pulls away from side of bowl. Turn out onto a lightly floured surface, and knead until smooth and elastic, about 5 minutes.

Place in an oiled bowl, turning to coat top, cover with plastic wrap, and let rise until doubled, about 1 hour. Punch down, cover, and let rise again until doubled (if using a sourdough starter, skip this rise). Turn out onto a lightly floured surface, and divide into 3 pieces. Shape into three loaves, and place on a baking sheet dusted with cornmeal. Cover with a cloth, and let rise until doubled.

Preheat oven to 400° F.

Cut shallow, diagonal slashes on tops of loaves. If using a pizza stone, slide dough onto preheated stone. For a crispier crust quickly but carefully mist loaves with water. Bake for about 30 minutes or until golden brown.

SUSAN'S RECOMMENDED READING

• Mary Gubser, *America's Bread Book: 300 Authentic Recipes for America's Homemade Breads, Collected on a 65,000-mile Journey through the Fifty United States* (New York: William Morrow and Company, 1985; New York: HarperTrade, 1992). This book has incredible variety, anecdotes about each recipe, and useful tips throughout.

• Christine Ingram and Jennie Shapter, *Bread* (London: Lorenz Books, 2003). If you need to see the pictures, this is your book. There are gorgeous photos throughout of both process and product, and many recipes are adapted for bread machines. Also included is an extensive history of bread and an illustrated guide to the breads of many different cultures.

• King Arthur Flour, *The King Arthur Flour Baker's Companion: The All-purpose Baking Cookbook* (Woodstock, VT: Countryman Press, 2003). This reference is authoritative and not limited to bread, with cool explanations of bread chemistry, techniques, and ingredients.

Ron Miller

THE MILLER RITUAL

When bread is wanting, all's to be sold.

BENJAMIN FRANKLIN, *Poor Richard's Almanac, 1733*

When Ron Miller was growing up in St. Paul in the 1930s and 1940s, his mother made it clear that her sons would not be coddled—and in the long run ill-served—by the stereotypes of the day. "She felt that boys needed to be able to take care of themselves," Ron recalled. So he learned how to sew on a button, how to iron a shirt, and how to operate the washing machine.

Ahead of her time, that woman. But she went even further. She let the elder Mr. Miller take over the kitchen on Sunday nights, ceding her territory to his enthusiasm. The result was that young Ron grew up knowing that it was OK for men to mess about with pots and pans and ovens.

But the even greater lesson was this: It's OK to follow your passion.

This well-rounded upbringing may help explain why Ron, now seventy-three, talks about making bread with an almost romantic effusiveness. "When I first baked bread, I loved it, loved it," he said. "I love baking bread. When I can't do it, I feel deprived. Even up at the lake, I bake."

Ron recalled quizzing his mother about the homely combination of flour, yeast, salt, and water, seeking certainty in a process that for her was the stuff of instinct. "I used to ask her, 'How do you know?' And she'd say, 'You'll know.' And eventually you do."

For Ron bread is not so much a culinary pursuit as a creative one. "I have a latent artistry thing, I guess, and this helps me let it out," he said. "And I find it therapeutic, especially the kneading. Sometimes when I'm angry, I'll just pound on it." More often, though, making bread is more like play. "I love the feel of kneading it. I suppose I'm going back to my infancy, when I loved to play in the mud."

Such a willingness to analyze, even rhapsodize, is a hallmark of our modern age yet seems perfectly suited to something as ancient as bread.

Ron, a real estate agent, began baking bread in earnest about twenty-three years ago. He's an experimenter. He likes toying with the steamed technique of a Boston brown bread or devising different combinations of fruits in a loaf. If a blizzard rolls in, that's a good day for making bagels, with their mixing, forming, rising, poaching, and glazing. He makes an imposing challah (HAA-la) for Jewish holy days, a swirling pinwheel that rises majestically.

But he also hews to the classic foundations of bread. It was during a class at the Dunwoody Institute, back when they offered such instruction, that he learned about making a poolish, a soupy starter that ferments overnight and boosts a dough's flavor.

"I'm always looking for ways to simplify the process," Ron said. "You know what they say: When an efficiency expert goes into a workplace, he looks for the laziest guy, because he knows that guy has found the easiest way to get the job done."

Hence, the Miller ritual:

Each Saturday, Ron gets up around 5 a.m. to mix his dough, incorporating his fragrant poolish from the night before into his mix. Then during the dough's first rise, and if it's the right season, he and his wife go to the St. Paul Farmers' Market. Upon their return he forms the loaves for their final swell. By lunchtime they're laying out the sausages, cheeses, and preserves they discovered at the market, preparing for their finale on a hunk of fresh-baked bread.

The farmers' market ritual is a microcosm of what he likes to do on vacation, poking around about the breads of the region or the country they're visiting. One reason he was elated to discover the St. Paul Bread Club was his hunch that it would be a community of shared recipes, shared passions, and shared exploration.

It is, but it's proven welcoming in another way. Newcomers often are surprised by the number of men, with gatherings almost evenly split between males and females. Does bread have a whiff of the macho? Or are these men just fully evolved?

I'm guessing that some of the appeal lies in how bread is one of the most physically involving foods to come out of most kitchens. As Ron said, "When people ask me what type of machine I use, I hold up my hands."

But there's something else about baking bread—an elemental quality to both the means and the end that successfully bridges the gender gap.

A fresh-baked loaf of bread, burnished and earthy and crackling with possibility, speaks to an innate yearning for romance that lies within us all. Among bread bakers this yearning just lies closer to the surface.

Rye Bread

This recipe was a prizewinner in the rye category at the bread club's 2004 baking contest. Ron prefers the crust that comes from using a baking or pizza stone that he's preheated in his oven. Instead of placing the formed loaves on a greased cookie sheet, sprinkle the sheet with cornmeal, which will let you slide the risen loaves onto the baking stone. **MAKES 2 OR 3 LARGE LOAVES OR 4 SMALL LOAVES.**

2	tablespoons active dry yeast
2	cups warm water
2	cups whole wheat flour
¼	cup honey
½	cup vinegar
1½	cups water
2½	cups rye flour
3 to 4	cups bread flour
1	heaping tablespoon salt
¾	cup bulgur
3	tablespoons caraway seeds

The night (or 6 to 8 hours) before baking, make a poolish by combining yeast, 2 cups water, and whole wheat flour in a medium bowl. Mix thoroughly, cover with plastic wrap, and let sit in a draft-free place.

The next day, combine poolish, honey, vinegar, and 1½ cups water. Stir in rye flour first and then 3 cups of bread flour, 1 cup at a time, until dough forms a ball. Add salt, and then turn out onto a lightly floured surface. Knead in bulgur, adding additional flour as needed. Knead in caraway seeds, adding flour until dough is only slightly sticky, 5 to 10 minutes. Place in a floured bowl, turning to coat top, cover with plastic wrap, and let rise until doubled, about 1 hour.

Punch down, knead slightly, and return to bowl. Cover and let rise for about 45 minutes. Turn out onto a lightly floured surface, and divide into desired number of loaves. Form and place on lightly oiled baking sheets. Cover with a cloth, and let rise for about 30 minutes or until doubled.

Preheat oven to 375° F.

Bake for 25 minutes, and then reduce heat to 350° F. Bake for another 20 to 25 minutes, depending on size of loaves. When done, loaves should sound hollow when tapped on bottom.

Holyday Challah

Challah is a delicious traditional Jewish loaf, eggy and honey scented. It also carries the wow factor of being easily shaped into pinwheels and many-stranded braids. This challah includes some whole wheat flour.

MAKES 1 VERY LARGE LOAF OR 2 MEDIUM LOAVES.

- ½ tablespoon active dry yeast
- 1 cup water
- 1 cup all-purpose flour
- ½ cup water
- ¾ cup honey
- 1 tablespoon olive oil
- 3 large eggs, lightly beaten
- 2½ to 3½ cups all-purpose flour
- 1 cup whole wheat flour
- ½ tablespoon salt
- 1 cup raisins or other dried fruit, if desired
- 1 large egg mixed with 1 teaspoon water for egg wash
  Poppy seeds or sesame seeds to scatter

The night (or 6 to 8 hours) before baking, make a poolish by combining yeast, 1 cup water, and 1 cup all-purpose flour. Mix thoroughly, cover with plastic wrap, and let sit in a draft-free place.

The next day, combine poolish, ½ cup water, honey, olive oil, and eggs in a large bowl. Mix in all-purpose and wheat flour 1 cup at a time until dough forms a ball. Add salt, and turn out onto a lightly floured surface. Knead until dough is smooth and springy, adding flour as needed, but no more than necessary. Dough should remain a bit sticky. If you want to add raisins or dried fruit, knead them in now. Place dough in a floured bowl, turning to coat top, cover with plastic wrap, and let rise until doubled, about 1 hour.

Punch down and knead to deflate bubbles, and then cover and let rise again for about 45 minutes. Turn out onto a lightly floured surface, kneading to deflate.

For a pinwheel shape of a holyday challah, roll into a long rope, and coil into a spiral shape on a baking sheet lined with parchment paper. Push up the center of the spiral a bit; it will rise to a "turban" shape.

To make a Sabbath challah shape, divide dough into 3 pieces, and cut ⅓ off each piece. Roll large pieces into strands, pinch together at top end, and braid, tucking ends under bottom. Roll small pieces into ropes, and braid together. Place small braid on top of larger braid, nestling firmly into place.

Cover and let rise for about 30 minutes or until doubled.

Preheat oven to 375° F.

Brush with egg wash and sprinkle with seeds. Bake for 20 minutes. Reduce heat to 350° F, and bake for 20 to 25 minutes, until loaf is golden brown and sounds hollow when tapped on bottom.

Honey Wheat Bread

The overnight poolish adds depth to the flavor of this wheat bread, and the cracked wheat adds texture. It provides a tasty foundation for whatever comes home from the farmers' market. **MAKES 3 LOAVES.**

- 1 tablespoon active dry yeast
- 2 cups water
- 2 cups whole wheat flour
- 1 cup honey
- 1 teaspoon canola oil
- 1 cup water
- 1 cup whole wheat flour
- 1 cup cracked wheat flour
- 4 to 5 cups bread flour
- 1 tablespoon salt

The night before baking, make a poolish by combining yeast, 2 cups water, and 2 cups whole wheat flour in a medium bowl. Mix thoroughly, cover with plastic wrap, and let sit in a draft-free place.

The next day, combine poolish, honey, oil, and remaining 1 cup of water in a large bowl. Add whole wheat flour and cracked wheat flour. Then add bread flour 1 cup at a time until dough forms a ball. Add salt, and turn out onto a lightly floured surface. Knead until smooth, elastic, and no longer sticky, adding additional flour as needed. Place in a floured bowl, turning to coat top, cover with plastic wrap, and let rise until doubled, about 1 hour.

Punch down and knead to deflate bubbles, and cover and let rise, about 45 minutes.

Preheat oven to 375° F.

Turn out onto a lightly floured surface, kneading to deflate, and divide into 3 pieces. Shape into loaves, and place in lightly greased bread pans. Cover with a cloth, and let rise until just doubled, about 30 minutes. Bake for 25 minutes. Reduce heat to 350° F, and bake for 20 minutes or until loaves sound hollow when tapped on bottom. Turn out of pans, and cool on wire racks.

Wheat, Wheat

This sturdy loaf is Ron's personal favorite, the result of longtime experimentation, with its variety of wheat in four forms. It took the top prize for wheat bread at the bread club's 2005 baking contest. **MAKES 2 LOAVES.**

½	tablespoon active dry yeast
1	cup water
1	cup whole wheat flour
1	cup water
¼	cup honey
¼	cup cracked wheat
½	cup wheat bran
¼	cup bulgur
½	tablespoon salt
1½	cups all-purpose flour

The night (or 6 to 8 hours) before baking, make a poolish by combining yeast, 1 cup water, and 1 cup whole wheat flour. Mix thoroughly, cover with plastic wrap, and let sit in a draft-free place.

The next day, combine poolish, 1 cup water, and honey. Add cracked wheat, bran, and bulgur, and mix well. Add salt and 1 cup flour, mixing until dough forms a ball. Turn onto a lightly floured surface, and knead in additional flour until slightly sticky. Place in a floured bowl, turning to coat top, cover with plastic wrap, and let rise, about 1 hour. Punch down and knead briefly, adding additional flour if needed, cover and let rise 45 minutes to an hour.

Preheat oven to 375° F.

Turn out onto a lightly floured surface, and shape into 2 loaves; place into greased bread pans. Cover with a cloth, and let rise until doubled, about 30 minutes. Bake for 20 minutes. Reduce heat to 350° F, and bake for another 20 minutes. When done, loaves should sound hollow when tapped on bottom. Turn out of pans, and cool on wire racks.

RON'S BAKING TIPS

· Making a poolish the night before greatly improves the flavor of the finished loaf because the long fermentation gives the yeast plenty of time to convert the dough's sugars.

· Buy yeast in bulk (look to your local co-op), and store it in the freezer. It's economical and will help ensure that you always have yeast on hand.

· I coat the bowl used for the bread's first rise with flour instead of oil. I don't like the feel of oil so I have tried to cut down on the amount I use. I put flour in the bowl and turn the dough in the flour to cover all of the bread. As I said before: I am lazy and it is easier to clean up flour than oil.

Klecko

JOYFULLY HONORING THE MASTERS

In the phrases of songs and poems . . . bread is gold. It is the motherland, it is the hard work of the masses, it is life itself.

TESTIMONY FROM A 1985 TRIAL IN WHICH A COLLECTIVE FARM MANAGER IN RUSSIA WAS CHARGED WITH FEEDING BREAD TO PIGS

It's time to tell you about Klecko.

When Dan McGleno was about as tall as a wheat stem, someone gave him Dr. Seuss's *My Book about Me,* in which kids could fill in facts about themselves and create the story of their lives. At the end there was a long list of future careers to choose among, but young Dan's ambition was nowhere to be found.

"So I wrote in, 'baker,'" he said. "I knew I was going to be a baker."

Years passed. Yet that early conviction held true. Dan McGleno the kid is now Klecko the baker (the story behind that name in a moment). In the world of banal job titles, he is production manager of the St. Agnes Baking Company in St. Paul. In the world of exuberant self-promotion, he is Lord of the Sourdoughs. In the world of the St. Paul Bread Club, he is its reason for being.

Klecko founded the club in 2003 for a couple of reasons. The first goes way back. As he tells it, he was a teenager heading down a fun but inevitably fruitless path when Tom Zolick got hold of him. Mr. Zolick, a Polish man who lived up the street, was a master baker who saw in this juvenile the potential for redemption.

Besides, the kid was begging him, although for reasons that wouldn't pass muster at your conventional culinary school: "The baking industry was kind of a nocturnal thing, and everyone seemed like a bunch of pirates," Klecko said, then grinned. "So I was attracted to that." His instruction began.

"I remember Master Zolick once telling me, 'If you were really smart, you'd get really good at this and get a TV show and teach housewives how to bake,'" Klecko said. "This was in the mid-1970s, you know, and he'd seen the first generation of women who stopped doing their own family baking. And while it was important for women to step up into the world, there was a loss."

(An aside: Klecko, now forty-three, still calls his teacher Master Zolick, upholding the formality of their master-apprentice relationship. Personal friendships within the Bakers' Guild were frowned upon. "They wanted you to come to the table and think about bread, not about going out for beers after work," Klecko said. "But it was all done with honor and respect.")

The idea for the bread club got a further nudge one Christmas Eve during his annual observance of an old Polish tradition of hanging loaves from a tree for the birds and the squirrels to enjoy. In Europe he would have been in some moonlit woodland; in St. Paul he was under the streetlights, adorning a tree in front of the Bean Factory, a neighborhood coffee shop.

The practice arose from the belief that bakers are supposed to give back to Christ by giving to the animals, but maybe humans could use some nurturing, too. "I started to see the power of baking." Master Zolick's vision of a TV show was reimagined as the St. Paul Bread Club.

Now, for the birth of "Klecko," we have to go back into the ethnic origins of St. Paul's bakeries. Once, local ovens were distinguished by whether they were run by Germans, Russians, Scandinavians, Irish, or Italians. When the large factory-sized bakeries came into being, the workers still divided themselves along ethnic lines.

So here came Daniel McGleno, freshly sprung from the baking curriculum at the Dunwoody Institute, into this world of fourth-, fifth-, and sixth-generation bakers. "In my whole life I'd never thought about anything other than baking bread," he said. "I had to show people how serious I was."

But he also needed to fit in. He was Polish on his mother's side and Irish on his father's but had grown up eating Polish bread, so he edged over toward the eastern European bakers. The trouble was they couldn't have someone with a name like McGleno in their midst. So they christened him Klecko, which, loosely translated, means "to revere your master."

He was in. Today, he's the heartbeat of St. Agnes, having remained through three changes of ownership, the current owners being Gary Sande and Larry Burns. He's developed his own potato-based sourdough starter that he calls a brick for its mass and heft. True to form, he gave it a name, "Annalisa," and true to her, he's kept her working away in huge vats for eighteen years.

If you've got a day or so to spare, Klecko will correct all the misconceptions you might have about sourdough. A good sourdough isn't defined by its sourness but by its density, which also enhances its moisture level. Too often what passes for sourdough today goes way beyond a subtle tang to having an almost acidic bite—as if you were eating baking soda.

Klecko's sourdoughs, even his step-it-up "nasty" varieties with their double dose of starter, are characterized by being both tender and dense, with an even crumb that literally tastes cool in your mouth.

Over the years, he's designed sourdough breads for dignitaries ranging from Ronald Reagan and Mikhail Gorbachev to the Archduke of Austria. This is the sourdough that provides the underpinning for the Saint Paul Hotel's black raisin bread, for the brat buns at the Xcel Energy Center, and for the breads that are served in dozens of local restaurants and entertainment centers, as well as being available at the farmers' markets in St. Paul and Minneapolis during the season.

Klecko has been generous enough to share recipes for some of his most well-known breads, including his classic sourdough, a Black Forest variation, a wild rice loaf, and an amazing cracker bread called *lavash* (la-VAHSH).

It's only fair to share, he said, because his own education continues with each bread club meeting. "In the early years of the business, you learn pretty fast to keep your mouth shut," he said, then laughed. "That's the real reason I founded the bread club, to have all these bakers to talk to."

Lavash

This is a showstopper at parties—a thin cracker as large as a baking sheet, striped with a pattern of seeds and spices, ready to be broken apart and nibbled. This cracker bread has been a staple in old-world countries for centuries, Klecko said, "but for years I could not get any chefs to touch this product. When Boston, L.A., New York, and Seattle started serving lavash in their cafés around 2001, I knew we were only a half year from accepting this." **MAKES 6 LAVASH.**

1	package active dry yeast
1¾	cups warm water
3½	cups whole wheat flour
3½	cups bread flour
1	tablespoon salt
2	large eggs beaten with 2 teaspoons water for egg wash
	Various toppings: sesame seeds, poppy seeds, paprika, cumin, or salt

Preheat oven to 375° F.

In a small bowl dissolve yeast in ¾ cup warm water, and set aside until foamy, about 5 minutes. In a large bowl combine whole wheat and bread flour. Add yeast mixture, and then slowly add remaining water, holding some back as you mix. You want the dough to resemble Silly Putty. Add salt, mixing well.

Turn out onto a lightly floured surface, and knead until dough is smooth. Divide into 6 pieces. Roll each piece with a rolling pin until as large as a cookie sheet yet paper thin. If dough pulls back on itself, stop occasionally and let gluten rest. Remember, thinness makes them *lavash;* size makes them impressive.

Carefully, place *lavash* on a baking sheet covered with parchment paper. Brush with egg wash, leaving some parts unwashed, which provides a color contrast. Sprinkle washed areas with sesame or poppy seeds. Experiment with other toppings, such as paprika, cumin, or salt. Bake for 10 minutes or until golden brown.

Sourdough Breads

A discussion of how to make a sourdough starter is worth its own book, and there are many excellent recipes detailed in a number of publications. In addition, you can order starters from several baking resources such as King Arthur Flour or use an Internet search engine to research sourdough sites. The recipes in this book make use of what bakers call a firm starter, as opposed to a liquid starter.

Brick Starter

If you'd like to try replicating Klecko's brick starter, here's his formula. Remember, though, that his "Annalisa" has been going for eighteen years, achieving a strength and complexity that a just-birthed starter won't have. But what do we have but time?

1½	cups water
1¾	cups bread flour
1¾	cups medium coarse pumpernickel rye flour
2	cups instant potato flakes

In a mixing bowl combine all ingredients and blend. This is a very stiff mixture that you may have to knead. Mix just until water is absorbed. Do not overmix. Place in a covered container, and let sit at room temperature undisturbed. After a few days it will soften considerably.

Begin a feeding schedule: Take 1 cup starter and knead into new mixture of original recipe. Do not overmix nor put potato flakes directly into water. Cover and let sit at room temperature until it begins to soften and swell, and then refrigerate until needed. Feed starter about once a week, beginning anew with 1 cup existing starter and discarding the rest.

Remember as you mix recipes to always leave at least 1 cup starter for your next batch.

Classic White Sourdough

2	packages active dry yeast
1½	cups warm water
¾	cup brick starter
4½	cups bread flour
1	tablespoon vinegar
2½	tablespoons salt

Dissolve yeast in ½ cup warm water, and set aside until foamy, about 5 minutes. Combine starter with remaining cup water to loosen somewhat, and then gradually add flour until dough comes together in a stiff ball. Add vinegar and salt, and continue mixing.

Turn out onto a lightly floured surface, and knead until smooth and elastic, about 10 minutes. Place in an oiled bowl, turning to coat top, cover with plastic wrap, and let rise until doubled, about1 hour.

Divide into 2 pieces, and shape into *batards* or *boules*. Place on baking sheet lined with parchment, make several slits across top, cover with a cloth, and let rise until doubled, about 1 hour.

Preheat oven to 450° F.

Bake 30 to 40 minutes or until loaf sounds hollow when tapped on bottom. Cool on wire rack.

Wild Rice Sourdough

"Back when Reagan and Gorby had their summit in the Twin Cities, my bake shop was commissioned to develop a bread that was indigenous to Minnesota. So we shipped wild rice down from the Leech Lake Wild Rice Company and got our grains and sweetening agents from local purveyors. Could it be possible that this symbolic loaf contributed to the end of the Cold War? I'd like to think so." **MAKES 4 LOAVES.**

2½ tablespoons active dry yeast
2¾ cups warm water
1⅓ cups brick starter
1 tablespoon molasses
¼ cup honey
2 tablespoons vinegar
2¼ cups whole wheat flour
6 cups bread flour
½ cup bran
2 tablespoons salt
1 cup cooked wild rice

In a large mixing bowl dissolve yeast in ¾ cup warm water, and let sit until foamy, about 5 minutes. Add remaining water, starter, molasses, honey, and vinegar, and mix well. Gradually, add whole wheat and bread flour, 1 cup at a time, reserving 1 cup. Add bran, salt, and wild rice, and mix well, adding additional flour as needed.

Turn out onto a lightly floured surface, and knead until smooth and elastic, about 10 minutes. Place in an oiled bowl, turning to coat top, cover with plastic wrap, and let rise until doubled, 1 to 2 hours.

Divide into 4 pieces, and shape into *batards* or *boules*. Place on baking sheet lined with parchment, make several slits across top, cover with a cloth, and let rise until doubled, about 1 hour.

Preheat oven to 450° F.

Bake 30 to 40 minutes or until loaf sounds hollow when tapped on bottom. Cool on wire rack.

Black Forest Sourdough

"When the Archduke of Austria came to host a national event at the Land-mark Center, I was asked to design an event bread that would capture the mood. This is my proudest effort. To this day, it's still served as the daily table bread at the Saint Paul Hotel." **MAKES 4 LOAVES.**

2	tablespoons active dry yeast
2¾	cups warm water
1⅓	cups brick starter
⅓	cup vinegar
2	tablespoons honey
4	tablespoons molasses
½	cup cocoa
7	cups bread flour
1¾	cups pumpernickel flour
3	tablespoons caraway seeds
2	tablespoons salt
2	cups raisins
1	egg beaten with 1 teaspoon water for egg wash

In a large mixing bowl dissolve yeast in ¾ cup warm water, and let sit until foamy, about 5 minutes. Add starter, remaining water, vinegar, honey, cocoa, and molasses, and mix well. Gradually, add pumpernickel and bread flour 1 cup at a time, reserving 1 cup. Add caraway seeds, salt, and raisins, and mix well, adding flour as needed.

Turn out onto a lightly floured surface, and knead until smooth and elastic, about 10 minutes. Place in an oiled bowl, turning to coat top, cover with plastic wrap, and let rise until doubled, 1 to 2 hours.

Divide into 4 pieces, and shape into *batards* or *boules*. Place on baking sheet lined with parchment, cover with a cloth, and let rise until doubled.

Preheat oven to 450° F.

Brush with egg wash, and make several slashes across top. Bake for 30 to 40 minutes or until loaf sounds hollow when tapped on bottom. Cool on wire rack.

Marie Wang

THE ART AND APPRECIATION

A loaf of bread, the Walrus said
Is what we chiefly need.
Pepper and vinegar besides
Are very good indeed.

LEWIS CARROLL, *Through the Looking Glass*

Marie Wang was describing her continuing quest to infuse bread with robust flavors when she laughed and confessed, "I'm not a very good midwesterner." And I could only wonder if she's the good midwesterner of the future.

What defines a good midwesterner anymore? The stereotypes are kept alive weekly on *A Prairie Home Companion* but also by the fact they still ring true. As long as there are people putting both butter and sour cream on their baked potatoes, boldly gilding the bland, the stable image of people taking satisfaction in basic foods will remain. This is not a bad thing.

But there is another midwesterner who navigates the aisles of grocery stores stocked with ingredients from Mexico, Cambodia, Vietnam, Somalia, and Italy. People from these countries now are good midwesterners, too, and they have shared their secrets.

"The pursuit of a new bread is a big part of what I love about baking," Marie said. A search for particular ingredients propels her from her Como Park home in St. Paul into far-flung neighborhoods with their ethnic groceries and family bakeries. "People have the recipes; you just have to go learn them."

I couldn't wait to see the recipe for her chipotle sourdough bread, which I'd tasted at the most recent club bake-off and then whistled when I saw the two teaspoons of catch-your-breath chipotle chili powder. Then she shared a recipe for baked puffed flatbread. These recipes were, as people here tend to say, something different.

Marie, thirty-three, is a second-generation Minnesotan. Her parents were born in China and raised in Taiwan, and she was born here while her father was attending graduate school at the University of Minnesota. Her mother almost always made traditional Chinese food, "the most amazing food." Yet each day around three, Marie finagled an invite to a friend's house to see if any of the bars, cookies, or breads that graced every Lutheran church cookbook were emerging from the oven.

"I've always loved baked goods," she said. She began baking while in elementary school; McCall's White Bread was her first recipe, a straightforward recipe that delivered the soft white bread that kids crave yet also hinted at the magic of transformation that awaited the more adventuresome baker.

Her serious romance with other foods blossomed in college when she began eating in a wide variety of restaurants. "I would be sitting there thinking, 'I bet I could make this,'" Marie said. The chemistry major inside her loved to puzzle out how the ingredients came together, and she began a long habit of reading the technique sections of cookbooks for pleasure.

Then someone gave her and her husband a bread machine for their wedding. They're clever things, these machines, but the magic happens out of sight, out of our reach. There's a time and a place for such convenience, but not if you truly enjoy the hands-on effort of making bread.

Effort? Maybe that's not the right word for a woman who refers to her kitchen as "my playground." Yet the fact remains that her kitchen also is a place where Kitchen Aid mixers go to die. Wang, who loves working with sturdy sourdoughs, has burned out four of them—"three of them the big guys," she said, with a barely veiled touch of pride. Fortunately, her other equipment needs are simple: parchment paper and a kitchen scale. Marie weighs all her flour and liquids for the greatest accuracy. "That's about it for gear," she said. "Bread is symbolic of simplicity."

Marie has made an evening ritual out of feeding her sourdough starter. Each night before bed, she takes a five-ounce portion of the firm brick from the fridge, works in flour and water to double it, and then sets it on the counter to develop for the next day's baking. The starter is from Klecko's eighteen-year-old starter, which she has combined with one of her own making. "When I began with the sourdough with its regular feeding schedule, everyone said, 'Oh, you're not really going to do that,' but I love it. It's therapeutic."

She mixes her breads in a sunlit corner of her kitchen. Along the ceiling is a tangled mural of morning glory vines that she has painted, a motif that crops up in odd nooks around the room. The flowers were prescient. One morning, she said, she was making bread and saw through the window a woman setting up her artist's easel in the alley. She watched her assemble her tubes and brushes, open her umbrella against the sun, and begin to paint. "It was just the most wonderful thing, to be making bread while watching a painting come to life."

And, as with art, appreciation is a subjective thing. Take the time that Marie proudly gave a loaf of sourdough to her parents.

"Their only comment was, 'That was a little sour, Marie.' When I tasted it, I realized what an understatement that was. I had unwittingly made really, really, really sour sourdough, but because they were good Chinese parents, they were ever so polite. I was horrified to realize that I had given the same batch to some friends that same week. What a surprise to hear back from them that they were ever so impressed with how wonderfully sour the bread was. Oh, to find the right audience for the mistakes!"

Marie tries to bake every day, and while she gives some away, her freezer is filled with loaves. "Now I know I'm going to die happy, with bread in both hands," she said, raising her arms high. "I bake enough to make sure that's going to happen!"

MARIE'S BAKING TIPS

• Get an oven thermometer, and check its readings against the oven gauge. Knowing your oven's accurate temperature makes a world of difference in your baking.

• Don't rely solely on recipes for baking times. Use the tips for knowing when baked goods are finished (e.g., skewer coming out clean, sounds hollow).

• If at all possible, measure ingredients by weight. It's more accurate and eliminates some of the variables in baking experiments.

• Bake as much as you possibly can. The smells in the house alone are worth it, let alone eating and enjoying the results.

Marie's Chipotle Sourdough

This densely textured loaf is the color of a sunset, making it a lively addition to a bread basket. It also won the sourdough sweepstakes ribbon at the bread club's 2005 baking contest. The chipotle powder—chipotles are smoke-dried chile peppers—lends a smoldering heat. Marie uses Klecko's brick sourdough starter, which calls for some planning ahead (see p. 40). Various sourdough starters also can be ordered by mail. Chipotle powder is available in co-ops, specialty stores, and some groceries. **MAKES 1 LARGE LOAF OR 2 SMALL LOAVES.**

> 1   cup brick starter
> 4½   to 5 cups bread flour
> 1½   cups warm water
> 2   teaspoons salt
> 2   teaspoons chipotle powder

Combine starter, flour, water, and salt, and mix at low speed in a stand mixer or by hand. When dough draws together and pulls clear of side of bowl, remove and knead by hand on a floured surface, about 10 minutes. Add chipotle powder, and knead until distributed throughout dough, about 5 minutes. Place in an oiled bowl, turning to coat top, cover with plastic wrap, and let rise until doubled, 2 to 3 hours.

Shape into *batard* or *boule*, and place on a wooden pizza peel or sheet pan generously sprinkled with cornmeal. Slash top of loaf several times. Cover with a cloth, and let rise for another 2 hours.

Preheat oven to 450° F.

Slide off peel or pan onto pizza stone or baking tiles, and bake for 15 minutes. Bread is best when baked on a stone or tiles, but you also can leave the loaves on the sheet pan to bake.

Baked Puffed Flatbread

Marie likes to fill these soft, sesame-speckled breads with chicken mango salad and serve them as wraps, but they also make great sopper-uppers for hummus and other dips. It's important to let the pieces of dough rest after forming them into balls and again after rolling them into four-inch circles. Otherwise, they will shrink and not hold their shape. This recipe originally was published in Cook's Illustrated. **MAKES 8 SIX- TO SEVEN-INCH BREADS.**

- 1 package active dry yeast
- 1 cup warm water
- 1 tablespoon olive oil, plus extra for brushing
- 2 teaspoons sugar
- ¼ cup plain yogurt
- 1½ teaspoons salt, plus extra for sprinkling
- ½ cup whole wheat flour, shaken through a wire strainer before measuring to remove coarse flakes of bran
- 2 cups bread flour
- 2 tablespoons sesame seeds (optional)

In either the work bowl of a food processor fitted with stainless steel blade or, if working by hand, a medium mixing bowl, sprinkle yeast over warm water. Add oil, sugar, and yogurt, and pulse to mix, about four 1-second bursts or, if working by hand, mix with a wooden spoon until combined well. Add salt, sieved whole wheat flour, and 2 cups bread flour; process until smoooth, about 15 seconds, scraping down sides of bowl as necessary or, if working by hand, mix with a wooden spoon until flour is incorporated, about 3 minutes.

Process dough (adding more flour as necessary just until dough pulls completely away from sides of bowl) until soft and satiny, about 30 seconds, or, if working by hand, turn dough out of mixing bowl onto very lightly floured work surface and knead until smooth and elastic, 12 to 15 minutes. Squeeze dough gently with full hand: if dough is sticky, sprinkle with flour and knead just to combine. Place dough in medium bowl or tall food storage container, cover with plastic wrap, and place in warm, draft-free spot until dough doubles in size, 30 to 45 minutes. (At this point dough can be punched down, wrapped tightly in plastic wrap, and refrigerated up to 2 days.)

Turn dough onto lightly floured work surface; sprinkle surface very lightly with flour if sticky. Cut dough into 8 pieces and form into balls. Cover and let rest for 5 minutes. With a rolling pin, roll each ball into a flat circle, about 4 inches in diameter. Cover and let rest again for 5 minutes. If using sesame seeds brush tops of circles lightly with water, sprinkle each circle with ¾ teaspoon seeds, and gently roll over with rolling pin once or twice so seeds adhere to dough.

About 30 minutes prior to cooking adjust oven rack to lowest position, line rack with unglazed baking tiles, pizza stone, or preheated baking sheet, and preheat oven to 500° F. Bake dough rounds on preheated tiles or pizza stone until bread is puffed and golden brown on bottom, 5 to 6 minutes. Transfer breads to wire rack to cool for 5 minutes; wrap in clean kitchen towels and serve warm or at room temperature.

Neapolitan-style Pizza Crust

This pizza crust is the thin, crisp, heat-blistered crust of pizza's origins in Naples, Italy. The key is a slow rise for the dough and a long preheat for the oven—plus a light hand with the toppings. This recipe is adapted from The Splendid Table. **MAKES 1 FIFTEEN-INCH PIZZA CRUST.**

> Generous ¼ teaspoon active dry yeast
> ½ cup warm water
> 1 teaspoon organic stone-ground all-purpose unbleached flour
> 1 to 1¼ cups organic stone-ground all-purpose unbleached flour
> ½ teaspoon salt
> Additional flour

In a medium bowl blend yeast, water, and 1 teaspoon flour, and set aside until foamy, about 5 minutes. Then blend in remaining flour and salt, forming a smooth, quite soft, slightly sticky dough. Turn out onto a lightly floured surface, and knead, about 5 minutes. Place in a large oiled bowl, cover with plastic wrap, and let stand in a cool place until doubled, about 1½ hours. If not ready to bake, keep dough covered, and hold up to 8 hours. About 20 minutes before baking, punch down, knead a few minutes, form into a ball, and cover.

Preheat oven to 500° F, setting rack to lowest position.

To make pizza, lightly oil a 14- to 16-inch pizza pan. Roll out dough as thin as possible, and spread over pan, rolling in edges to form a rim. Let rest 10 minutes. Top as desired, and bake 10 minutes. Then using a spatula and a thick oven mitt, pull out the oven rack, slip the pizza off the pan and onto the oven rack, slide rack back into place, and bake 2 minutes. Remove pie by slipping it back onto pan. Serve immediately.

Pizza Margherita

1 tablespoon extra-virgin olive oil
½ medium onion, minced
1 sprig parsley, chopped
1 large clove garlic, minced
¼ teaspoon dried oregano
1½ cups canned whole peeled tomatoes
⅓ cup packed fresh basil leaves, torn
3 ounces fresh mozzarella in liquid, thinly sliced
2 to 3 tablespoons extra-virgin olive oil
Salt and freshly ground black pepper

In a 10-inch skillet heat 1 tablespoon olive oil over medium heat. Sauté onion and parsley until golden, and then stir in garlic and oregano for a few seconds. Add tomatoes, crushing them as they go into the pan (resist the temptation to substitute crushed tomatoes). Boil, stirring often, for 5 minutes or until thick.

Spread sauce over a rolled-out crust, sprinkle with basil, mozzarella, and, finally, the oil. Finish with a generous grind of black pepper and a little salt. Bake as directed in pizza crust recipe.

Ricotta Pancakes

Pancakes actually are a variety of flatbread, and these push the definition further by incorporating ricotta cheese into the batter. Marie says the difference is subtle but tasty. Beating the egg whites separately makes an exceptionally light and fluffy pancake. Panzano at the Monaco Hotel in Denver, Colorado, happily shared this mainstay of their breakfast menu.

MAKES ABOUT 40 SMALL PANCAKES.

4	large eggs, separated
2	cups ricotta cheese
⅔	cup sour cream
1⅓	cups all-purpose flour
1	tablespoon baking powder
½	teaspoon salt
½	teaspoon baking soda
1½	cups whole milk
	Melted unsalted butter
	Maple syrup

In a large bowl whisk together yolks, ricotta, and sour cream. In another large bowl mix flour, baking powder, salt, and baking soda. Add flour mixture to yolk mixture, and stir until combined. Stir in milk.

In another large bowl beat whites with an electric mixer on medium speed until soft peaks form. Gently, fold beaten whites into batter. Heat griddle or large skillet over medium heat. Brush with butter. Working in batches, spoon 2 tablespoons batter onto griddle for each pancake. Cook until golden brown, about 3 minutes per side. Serve with maple syrup.

MARIE'S RECOMMENDED READING

- Harold McGee, *On Food and Cooking: The Science and Lore of the Kitchen,* rev. ed. (New York: Scribner, 2004). While not a cookbook, this book is an incredible resource for understanding the history and the science behind food.

Pat Roberts

HONORING OUR GRANDMOTHERS

Bread is better than the song of birds.

DANISH PROVERB

Growing up on the Iron Range, Pat Roberts knew how tight-lipped some women could be about their fillings for the strudel-like spiral of yeast bread called *potica* (po-TEET-sa). Any grandmother arriving from eastern Europe would have carried her recipe for the rich paste of ground nuts and sugar like a treasure—an heirloom for daughters to absorb over a childhood of baking.

So when a mining-related company transferred the Robertses and several other families from Minnesota to Colorado, Pat knew what she had to do. First, she gently scolded the younger women to stop their homesick fretting and to realize that they were capable of re-creating their families' Christmas traditions: "Just because your grandmother isn't here doesn't mean you can't have potica."

Then she announced that she would teach them how to make the bread, which led to a second far more grave announcement: she would not pry into their families' secrets. "I'll give you all the tips I know, but you don't have to tell me your recipe." She knew that they'd have to write home for instructions that, despite having crossed an ocean, probably had never left Grandma's head.

"People are very particular about their potica," Pat said, recalling those days. She makes it the way her father liked it, meaning that the spiral of eggy, buttery dough bakes to invisibility, becoming a mere rumor between the layers of ground nuts. "He always said if you want to eat coffee cake, eat coffee cake."

In a Rosemount home as neat and compact as she is—and whose front yard boasts a boulder of taconite as hefty as a hog—Pat moved quickly. Over the dining room table she spread a clean bed sheet long ago reserved for potica days. With deft confidence and fingers free of jewelry, she pulled a bowlful of dough into an expanse as thin as a cobweb and then lobbed dollops of walnut filling over it all. Her family's recipe is for a purist's potica with no raisins, no cinnamon.

"What about ground almonds?" I asked, telling her how one of my husband's Slovenian aunts in Cleveland favored such a filling, further embellished with golden raisins. Pat glanced up and then shook her head. Nothing more was said.

Not that she was passing judgment, exactly. Walnuts, almonds, cinnamon, whatever—the important thing is that people feel a connection to their breads, a connection so secure that they share it freely with others. For as long as she could remember, Pat grew up experiencing the unique intimacy of a bequeathed formula of flour and yeast.

Her potica recipe came from Grandma Samarzja. Pat learned to bake the Finnish cardamom braid from Irene Nikunen and the Italian focaccia from Elvi Frisbee and her mother, Josie Sacripant. Then there's the Norwegian coffee cake from Mrs. Kutz. Pat laughed, suddenly realizing the social amber in which some people forever are suspended. "I have no idea what her first name was; she was always Mrs. Kutz."

Through these women she learned to make the breads that graced the tables of Buhl, a mining town halfway between Virginia and Hibbing in northern Minnesota. You want to know the depth of Pat's roots? Her grandmother lived in the seventh tent put up in town.

Pat's father worked in the mines, as did her father-in-law, as did her husband. She taught home economics for a few years and then raised a family. Eventually, they moved to Rosemount, where she uses her food knowledge writing chemical specifications for a food service company.

Always, she's baked bread. Pat's mixing bowl is a White Mountain bread machine that resembles an ice cream churn. The wooden bucket holds dough enough for four loaves. Years ago, she got it for $30 and uses it every week.

Pat says she bakes bread so she can give it away, but it's pretty clear that giving it away is what enables her to bake more bread. "People feel better if they're acknowledged."

This may help explain the role of potica in so many families of eastern European stock, who know the effort it asks of a baker. On the Range, Pat said, they claimed, "If you don't have potica when you're married or buried, it hasn't happened."

They know the wonder that this supple dough inspires as it's coaxed to the very edges of an old sheet slightly tinged with walnut stains. This bread of generations past helps affirm the present.

Walnut Potica

Don't be put off by the length of this recipe. While you may wish you had Pat at your side as you begin to pull the dough, you'll be amazed by how pliable it is. Fresh, dry flour gives the dough its greatest elasticity, so Pat always starts this recipe by opening a new bag. Making potica is a communal thing, far more enjoyable and easier with two or three others helping ease the dough across the tabletop. **MAKES 5 TO 6 LOAVES.**

Dough

- 1½ cups lowfat milk
- ½ cup sugar
- ½ cup unsalted butter (1 stick), room temperature
- 1 package active dry yeast
- 1 teaspoon salt
- 2 large eggs, beaten
- 5 to 6 cups bread flour

Filling

- ½ cup unsalted butter
- 1½ cups lowfat milk
- 2 cups granulated sugar
- ½ scant cup honey
- 2½ pounds English walnuts, about 10 cups
- 4 large eggs, beaten
- ½ cup unsalted butter, melted

Heat milk to 120° F. In the bowl of a mixer, combine sugar and butter. Add milk, and mix until combined. Add yeast, salt, and beaten eggs, and mix. With mixer running, add flour, 1 cup at a time, but not more than 5 cups. Dough should be soft to moderately firm, not stiff. If kneading with a dough hook, knead about 15 minutes, or, if by hand, 30 minutes, adding flour sparingly. Dough should be elastic and have air bubbles no larger than ¼ inch. Place dough in a lightly oiled bowl, turning to coat top, cover with plastic wrap, and let rise in a warm, draft-free place until doubled, about 2 to 3 hours. Be patient; this dough doesn't like to be rushed.

Using a food processor and working in small batches, grind nuts until uniformly fine, being careful not to grind to a paste. Heat milk in a Dutch oven or other large, heavy pan, preferably cast iron. Add butter until melted, and then add walnuts, sugar, and honey. Stir over medium heat until mixture boils. Don't let it scorch! Temper eggs by whisking in small amount of boiling mixture, and then add tempered eggs to nut mixture. Cook for 30 minutes over low heat, stirring frequently. Don't let it scorch! Set aside until dough has risen.

Preheat oven to 350° F.

Take a large, clean piece of fabric—an old sheet or a tablecloth—and spread over a large table, taping edges under table, making a smooth, unmoving surface. Flour generously. Take off any rings or bracelets. Place dough in middle of table, and using fingertips, pull dough from underneath, slowly stretching toward table edges. Take your time. If a hole appears, don't patch it. Keep pulling until dough is as thin as onionskin. It will cover an area about five feet long by three feet wide.

Spread ½ cup melted butter over dough. Next, using a spatula, drop dollops of nut filling all over dough, and gently spread until entire surface is covered with a very thin coating. Cut off any thick edges of dough.

Remove tape, and holding on to cloth, lift one long edge, using it to roll dough into a long cylinder. (Make sure it doesn't roll off the other side of the table.) Lay five or six greased 8½-by-4½-inch loaf pans along roll for a guide, and then with the edge of a teacup saucer (a saucer seals the ends better than a knife cut can), cut dough into pan-sized lengths. Place each piece seam side down in a pan. Prick each piece four times with a fork.

Bake on middle rack of oven for 15 minutes. Turn oven down to 325° F, lightly cover loaves with aluminum foil, and bake for 40 to 50 minutes. When done, loaves should be medium to dark brown and loose when pan is lightly shaken. Do not underbake. Remove from pans, and cool on a wire rack.

These freeze well if tightly wrapped in plastic wrap and aluminum foil.

Swedish Rye Bread

This loaf is delicately flavored, lighter than many rye breads, and terrific for sandwiches. **MAKES 4 LOAVES, BUT THE RECIPE IS EASILY HALVED.**

2	tablespoons active dry yeast
½	cup warm water
½	cup light brown sugar
½	cup light molasses
2	tablespoons salt
4	tablespoons shortening
3	cups hot water
5	cups medium rye flour (not stone-ground)
6½ to 7	cups all-purpose flour
2	tablespoons caraway seeds (optional)

Dissolve yeast in warm water, and set aside until foamy, about 5 minutes. In a large bowl combine sugar, molasses, salt, shortening, and hot water, stirring until shortening is dissolved. Add caraway seeds at this point if desired. Mix in rye flour. Let mixture cool slightly, and add yeast. Add white flour 1 cup at a time, stirring with a wooden spoon or hands until dough has a soft to medium consistency. Turn onto a floured board, and knead until smooth and elastic, about 10 to 15 minutes.

Place in an oiled bowl, turn to coat top, cover with plastic wrap, and leave in a warm place until doubled, about 1 to 2 hours. Turn out onto a floured surface, and shape into 4 round loaves. Place on 2 greased baking sheets, cover with a cloth, and let rise until doubled, about 1 to 2 hours. Preheat oven to 375° F.

Bake for 35 to 40 minutes until golden brown. To soften crusts, wipe loaves with a bit of shortening after baking.

Finnish Cardamom Bread

This beautifully pale golden loaf is lightly scented with cardamom seeds that Pat grinds in a coffee grinder, and has just a whisper of sweet glaze. The braided top on a conventional loaf shape is striking. **MAKES 2 LOAVES.**

1	tablespoon active dry yeast
¼	cup warm water
½	teaspoon sugar
1	cup lowfat milk
2	large eggs, beaten
½	cup sugar
½	teaspoon salt
½	teaspoon crushed cardamom seeds
4½	cups bread flour, divided into three parts
¼	cup unsalted butter, room temperature
1	beaten egg for glaze
	Granulated sugar for sprinkling

Mix yeast, warm water, and sugar until yeast is dissolved. Set aside. Heat milk in a saucepan over low heat until small bubbles appear along edges, and then cool to about 120° F. Add beaten eggs, sugar, salt, cardamom, and 3 cups flour. Beat well. Add butter, and beat well. Add yeast mixture and then remaining flour in thirds, mixing until dough has a soft to medium consistency. Knead on a lightly floured surface or with a dough hook until smooth and elastic, about 10 minutes, adding as little additional flour as possible.

Turn into an oiled bowl, turning to coat top, cover with plastic wrap, and let rise until almost doubled, about 1 to 2 hours. Punch down dough, and let rise once more until almost doubled, about 1 hour.

Turn out onto a lightly floured surface, and divide into 6 pieces. Take 3 pieces, roll each into a rope, and braid together to form a loaf. Repeat with remaining 3 pieces. Place loaves on a greased baking sheet or in greased 8½-by-4½-inch loaf pans. Cover with a cloth, and let rise until doubled, about 45 minutes.

Preheat oven to 375° F.

Brush with beaten egg, and sprinkle with sugar. Bake for 25 minutes or until loaf sounds hollow when tapped on bottom. Invert from pan, and cool on wire rack.

Focaccia

Pat won in the Italian breads category at the St. Paul Bread Club's 2005 baking contest with this focaccia (fo-CAH-cha) recipe passed to her by Josie Sacripant. Josie's parents immigrated to Minnesota from Naples in 1901, and at Ellis Island her Italian mother, Anna Mone, was renamed "Anna Mooney," an Irish name that, fortunately, had no effect on her baking traditions. **MAKES 1 LARGE ROUND.**

1	package active dry yeast
1	cup warm water
1	tablespoon sugar
2	tablespoons extra-virgin olive oil
4	tablespoons canola oil
½	teaspoon salt
2½	to 2¾ cups all-purpose flour
	Olive oil for brushing
	Chosen toppings (e.g., Italian herbs, salt, freshly grated Parmesan cheese)

In large bowl dissolve yeast in warm water, and set aside. Combine sugar, oils, and salt, and then add to yeast mixture. Add 2 cups flour, and mix well. Then slowly add remaining flour. Knead on a lightly floured counter with hands or, if too sticky, with a dough hook, or stir and stretch with a wooden spoon in mixing bowl, about 5 minutes. Place dough in an oiled bowl, turn to coat top, cover with plastic wrap, and let rise until doubled, about 1 to 2 hours.

Turn dough onto greased sheet pan, and gently press into a large circle. Cover with a cloth, and let rise until light and full of air, about 45 minutes.

Preheat oven to 375° F.

Brush with olive oil, and sprinkle with chosen toppings—Pat uses a tomato, basil, and pesto seasoning (look in your grocer's seasonings or Italian foods aisle); kosher salt; and freshly grated Parmesan cheese. Bake for 30 to 35 minutes or until golden brown.

PAT'S BAKING TIPS

· I am careful to use fresh bread flour so that the opened flour hasn't had a chance to pick up moisture from humid air. I've noticed that the gluten develops better and the dough stretches more easily when fresh flour is used and when the humidity is low.

· When I place the dough in a bowl to rise, I prefer to use the same bowl each time so that I can easily tell when it's doubled.

Bill Middeke

A BREAD BAKER, FINALLY

Bread is like dresses, hats, and shoes—in other words, essential!

EMILY POST

People wonder when Bill Middeke finds the time to bake bread. Men are especially skeptical. "They think if you start some bread, you have to be here with it the whole time," Bill said. "I do part of it, then go out and mow the lawn. Then come in, do the next step, then go do something else. You're not tied to the kitchen."

Bread making often is thought of as fussy and old-fashioned, a long-odds collaboration of yeast, time, and expertise. In fact, the process is quite logical and far more flexible than most imagine. And then there's the whole anger management thing.

"I make my best bread when I'm mad," Bill said. "You know, when you've had one of those 'You want it when?!' days at the office, I come home and," he said as he jabs a fist into an imaginary bowl, "kapow!"

A vigorous session of kneading has a steadying rhythm that can overcome the most chaotic day. A good yeasty dough can handle all the stress you can dish out—even is the better for it. The mass changes under your touch, absorbs your anger. The dough becomes easier to work with. You become easier to live with.

"I like the process," Bill said. "I don't own a bread machine, and I don't anticipate getting one. I like hand kneading, and until it comes to the point where I can't, I will."

Bill, fifty-nine, didn't set out to make bread, not the first time anyway. Rather, the task was thrust upon him. This was back in St. Louis, Missouri, some thirty-five years ago, when he was a senior in college. His grandmother was preparing to go into the hospital when she realized that a small cake of compressed yeast in her refrigerator would go bad before she returned—no small consequence in her mind.

"Being a good German hausfrau and not wanting anything to go to waste, she gave it to my mother and said, 'Make something,'" Bill recalled. "So my mother turned around and gave it to me and said, 'Make something.' So I did."

It wasn't a tough sell. Bill had grown up inhaling deeply whenever he'd drive past the big factory for the Tastee Baking Company. "I've always loved the smell of bread," he said. "I think I could get up from a Thanksgiving dinner, smell fresh-baked bread, and sit down and eat again."

Yet years would pass before he defined himself as a bread baker. "After I got married, I'd get the urge to bake every once in awhile. But then the kids came along, and they always wanted store-bought bread."

His kids and millions of others. Almost all of the bakers in this book told a similar story. Despite the artisanal wheats and baguettes and the whole grain marvels being pulled from ovens, their kids pleaded for rectangular pillows with names like Tastee and Wonder and Holsum. The ease with which such breads could be rolled into doughy pills explains only a part of their appeal. Maybe soft and white simply is a comforting combination whether in the form of ice cream or down pillows or sandwich bread.

In any case, although Bill baked less and less often, he never completely stopped. For years he's been tinkering with the recipe for Beer Rye Bread, the original newspaper clipping from the now-defunct *St. Louis Globe-Democrat* more keepsake than resource. Same with a loaf he calls Birdseed Bread, an inspiration that came to him while he and friends took part in a bike ride from Amsterdam to Paris in order to raise money for AIDS research.

"They have great breads over there, and we ate tons of these rolls that were loaded with all these crunchy seeds," he said. "After we got back here, a friend asked if I could make some more of those rolls. I told her I wished she would have asked me when we were over there. I would have paid closer attention to what was in them!"

He set out trying to re-create them, settling on a blend of poppy, sesame, sunflower, pumpkin, flax, millet, amaranth, and caraway seeds. But he keeps changing the mix, depending on what he feels like—or has on hand.

Bill considers himself a bread baker now, although his job in information technology systems pays the bills. He raises money for his church by offering bidders a loaf-a-month deal. He's wowed a few picnic crowds with his Italian loaf—a huge wreath into which he weaves fat sausages and eggs that bake together to a golden lunch.

But it's by his stollen that he is known. Starting in October, weekends in his Eden Prairie kitchen are spent kneading batches of the eggy, rum-scented bread rich with preserved fruit and citrus peel. By the time the holidays are over, he's handed over more than 120 stollen to friends, neighbors, and other worthy souls. Some even get the story:

Stollen is a German Christmas bread dating back to the year 1400. People in Dresden wanted a bread to celebrate Christ's birth and came up with a folded shape to resemble the baby Jesus in swaddling cloths. But the Pope had banned the luxuries of butter and milk during Advent, leaving only flour, oats, and water.

This made a rather wretched loaf, so Ernst of Saxony beseeched the Pope to lift the ban. The Pope replied favorably in what became known as "the butter letter," in which he said that, for a small fee, the ingredients could be used with a clear conscience and God's blessing.

The floodgates of temptation thus opened, candied fruits were not far behind.

German Christmas Stollen

The distinctive folded shape of this traditional holiday bread is meant to symbolize the baby Jesus wrapped in swaddling cloths. Bill adapted this recipe from his 1973 edition of Better Homes and Gardens Homemade Bread Cook Book. **MAKES 2 STOLLEN.**

1 cup brown raisins
½ cup chopped and mixed candied fruits and peels
¼ cup dark rum
4 to 4½ cups all-purpose flour
2 packages active dry yeast

1 cup lowfat milk
½ cup unsalted butter
¼ cup sugar
1 teaspoon salt
2 large eggs
½ teaspoon almond extract
2 tablespoons grated orange peel
1 tablespoon grated lemon peel
½ cup chopped pecans or almonds
3 tablespoons lowfat milk
2 cups powdered sugar, sifted

Soak raisins and mixed candied fruits and peels in rum. In large mixer bowl combine 1½ cups of flour and yeast. Heat milk, butter, sugar, and 1 teaspoon salt in saucepan until warm, stirring constantly to melt butter. Add to dry mixture with eggs, almond extract, and citrus peels.

Beat at low speed with electric mixer for half a minute, scraping bowl. Beat 3 minutes at high speed. By hand, stir in fruit and rum mixture, nuts, and enough remaining flour to make a soft dough. Knead on a floured surface until smooth, about 8 minutes. Place in an oiled bowl, turning to coat top, cover with plastic wrap, and let rise until doubled.

Punch down dough, and divide in half. Cover and let rest 10 minutes. Roll each half into a 10-by-7-inch oval. Fold one long side over to within ½ inch of opposite side, and seal edge by gently pressing together. Place on a greased baking sheet, cover with a cloth, and let rise until doubled.

Preheat oven to 375° F.

Bake for about 15 to 20 minutes. While warm, glaze with confectioners' icing made by whisking 3 tablespoons milk into 2 cups powdered sugar, adding additional milk by the teaspoon to get a spreadable consistency. Or omit glaze and dust heavily with powdered sugar. Garnish with candied fruits.

Birdseed Bread

Slicing into this nubbly bread reveals a gorgeous mosaic of seeds and textures. Bill is always fiddling with the combination of seeds and urges bakers to adjust the mixture to suit their own tastes. For a less dense loaf, use milk in place of some of the water. **MAKES 2 LOAVES.**

2	cups warm water
1	tablespoon active dry yeast
1	tablespoon salt
1½	tablespoons vegetable oil
¼	cup honey
1	large egg, beaten
2	cups whole wheat flour
1	generous tablespoon each of poppy, sesame, sunflower, pumpkin, flax, millet, and amaranth seeds or a combination of your choice to make about ¾ to 1 cup total
1	tablespoon caraway seed, if desired
3	to 3½ cups all-purpose flour

In large mixing bowl combine warm water and yeast, stirring to dissolve. Let stand until foamy, about 5 minutes. Stir in salt, oil, honey, and beaten egg. Add whole wheat flour, 1 cup at time, beating until smooth. Stir in seeds.

Add white flour until you have soft, workable dough. It will be on the sticky side, but try not to add more flour than necessary. Turn out onto a floured surface, and knead until smooth and elastic, about 10 minutes.

Place in an oiled bowl, turning to coat top, cover with plastic wrap, and let rise until doubled, about 1 to 2 hours. Punch down, and form into 2 loaves. Place into greased loaf pans, cover with a cloth, and let rise until doubled.

Preheat oven to 350° F.

Bake for about 55 minutes or until loaves sound hollow when thumped on bottom. Turn out of pans, and cool on a wire rack.

100 Percent Whole Wheat Bread

Using a stone-ground flour will enhance this firm bread's nutritive value and create a nuttier flavor. But use a light hand! With whole wheat flour the dough can quickly became stiff and unworkable. This is from Mary's Bread Basket and Soup Kettle *by Mary Gubser.* **MAKES 1 LOAF.**

1 package active dry yeast

⅓ cup warm water

¼ cup unsalted butter

1 teaspoon salt

⅓ cup boiling water

½ cup honey or light molasses, divided

⅓ cup nonfat dry milk

⅔ cup water

3 to 3½ cups stone-ground whole wheat flour

Make a sponge by sprinkling yeast over warm water in a small bowl, stirring until dissolved; set aside until foamy, about 5 minutes. In a medium bowl combine butter, salt, boiling water, and ¼ cup honey or molasses. Blend thoroughly. Add dry milk and ⅔ cup water. Stir in yeast mixture. Mix in 1 cup flour, beating until smooth. Cover with a towel, and set in a warm place until doubled, about 30 minutes.

When sponge has doubled, blend in remaining ¼ cup honey or molasses and enough remaining flour to make a soft dough. Be careful to add no more flour than necessary. Turn out onto a lightly floured surface, and knead until smooth and elastic, about 10 to 15 minutes, brushing hands with flour when needed. Place dough in an oiled bowl, turning to coat top, cover with plastic wrap, and let rise until doubled, about 1½ hours.

Punch down dough, shape into a loaf, and place in a greased loaf pan. Cover with a cloth, and let rise until dough curves over top of pan, about 1 hour.

Preheat oven to 350° F.

Bake for 55 minutes or until loaf sounds hollow when tapped on bottom. Turn out onto a wire rack to cool, brushing with melted butter if desired.

Beer Rye Bread

This bread bakes to a gorgeous burnished brown color and is rich with the scents of molasses and orange. This recipe, from the St. Louis Globe-Democrat *in Bill's hometown, originally called for ⅓ cup lard or bacon fat. Bill uses—sigh—shortening.* **MAKES 4 SMALL LOAVES,** *each the right size for a family meal.*

  3 cups beer
  ⅓ cup shortening
  ½ cup firmly packed light brown sugar
  ½ cup light molasses
1½ tablespoons salt
  2 tablespoons grated orange peel
  2 tablespoons caraway seeds
  2 packages active dry yeast
  ½ cup warm water
  5 cups unsifted rye flour
  5 to 6 cups unsifted all-purpose flour

BILL'S BAKING TIPS

• Use ingredients at room temperature. I buy flour in twenty-five-pound bags and keep it in the freezer. Then I let it come to room temperature before using. Using frozen flour slows the rising process.

• Make sure you don't kill the yeast by using liquid that's too warm. I use what I call the finger method. If the liquid is too hot to leave a finger in for a few seconds, it's too hot for the yeast.

• If your dough rises too long and collapses, knead it lightly and form the loaves again, cover, and let rise.

• Make sure you have all your ingredients before you start. Running to the store in the middle of making bread is a pain.

Heat beer in a saucepan over medium heat until barely bubbling. Add shortening, brown sugar, molasses, salt, orange peel, and caraway seeds. Cool to lukewarm.

In a small bowl dissolve yeast in warm water. Wait until foamy, about 5 minutes, and then add to lukewarm beer mixture. Beat in rye flour and enough white flour to make a soft dough. Turn out onto a heavily floured surface, and knead until smooth and elastic, about 10 minutes. Place in a greased bowl, turning to coat top, cover with plastic wrap, and let rise in a warm place until doubled, about 2 hours.

Punch down dough, and divide into 4 pieces. Form each into a round shape or a long oval. Place on a greased baking sheet, and slash tops with a sharp knife. Cover with a cloth, and let rise until doubled, about 45 minutes.

Preheat oven to 350° F.

Bake for 40 to 45 minutes. Let cool on wire racks.

BILL'S RECOMMENDED READING

• Mary Gubser, *Mary's Bread Basket and Soup Kettle* (New York: HarperTrade, 1985). This was one of my early cookbooks. The binding is getting a bit tattered, and some of the pages are speckled from spills. I use it a lot.

• Bernard Clayton, *Bernard Clayton's New Complete Book of Breads* (New York: Simon & Schuster, 2003). I like this book because of its wide vari-

ety of breads and its easy-to-follow recipes. Plus, it tells you how much time each step will take.

• Judith Olney, *Judith Olney on Bread* (New York: Random House, 1985). I like to use this one when I'm making bread for a special occasion. There's a recipe for rolls that you assemble like a bunch of grapes, and I like to take the Italian picnic loaf to group functions.

Char Johnson

A BREAD EDUCATION

Bread is the warmest, kindest of words. Write it always with a capital letter, like your own name.

A SIGN SIGHTED IN A RUSSIAN CAFÉ, 1985

A half century ago Char Johnson married into baking, although she didn't know it at the time. Her own mother baked maybe two or three times a year, mostly when there was a celebration that called for some fussing. For the holidays there would be a coffee cake from a recipe from her German homeland or raised doughnuts.

So during the first few years of Char's marriage to Rollie, bread came in a bag. Then they moved from Ohio to Minnesota, where Rollie grew up and where, more to the point, his mother's baking was as much a part of the day as making coffee.

His mom baked all the time, turning out a dozen or more loaves at a shot. "She had a huge, huge stainless steel bowl," Char said. So when the couple settled in the Twin Cities in 1956, Char decided to become a student. Her mother-in-law proved a generous teacher. As with the best of educations, the knowledge came gradually but steadily, its principles corroborated by experience.

"I'd ask her how she did this or how she did that, and she'd tell me everything she thought I should know," Char said. "She made the most amazing sweet rolls. One of her tricks was to pour cream over the dough in the pan just before she put it in the oven."

My eyebrows must have shot up, for Char gave me a reassuring look. "Oh, you don't need a lot of cream," she said, "maybe a quarter cup drizzled over. It makes them so moist. And half-and-half will do, too."

Apparently so, for Char has made it to seventy-five. Her mother-in-law passed on long ago, but her work lives on in the fresh scones Char bakes for breakfast and the banana bread that appears whenever the bananas outlast the grandchildren on their frequent visits to Vadnais Heights. And true to someone who's learned at another's elbow, she bakes by feel and instinct.

"I don't have a particular recipe," she said. "I just go for it. Even a recipe that I'm following, I'll end up winging it." Still, she has some guidelines. For instance, her mother-in-law taught her never to use more than one cup of whole wheat flour per loaf or it will be too dense. And she determines the amount of liquid to use by the quantity she wants to bake. "If I want four loaves of bread, then I use four and a half cups of water. Or if I have some leftover buttermilk, I'll use that as part of my liquid."

The flour follows, measured by feel and logic. That's just as well, perhaps, because if a Minnesota Gophers football game is on the air, no recipe card is going to get more than a cursory glance.

Char bakes for her kids and for their kids. She bakes for friends and neighbors. But she also bakes for herself. "I need to take my frustrations out in the kneading," she said, laughing, but only just barely.

Yet in some ways, she also bakes for her mother-in-law, whose influence still is felt, most spectacularly in the deep red fifty-gallon lard can emblazoned with the logo for Iowana Brand that she bequeathed to Char. It makes a perfect flour bin.

She also uses her mother-in-law's bread tins—tins that have been greased and fired for 100 years. "They're so well seasoned," Char said, and then, caught in a memory, she added, "She remembered back when bread was twelve cents a loaf."

Was twelve cents a bargain or luxury? Then, as now, it depends upon your circumstances. I'm thinking, though, that the price of bread was nothing compared with the priceless gift of having a daughter-in-law who was a willing, even grateful, pupil.

French Bread

There are artisanal baguettes with great holes and crackling crusts, and there is comfort food. This is the latter, a lovely firm, white loaf.
MAKES 2 LOAVES.

2	tablespoons active dry yeast
2	cups warm water
¼	cup sugar
1½	tablespoons vegetable oil
1	tablespoon salt
5½	cups all-purpose flour
1	egg white, beaten

In a large bowl dissolve yeast in warm water, and let sit until foamy, about 5 minutes. Add sugar, oil, and salt, and mix well. Gradually, add flour until dough comes together in a mass. Turn out onto a lightly floured surface, and knead until smooth and springy. Place in an oiled bowl, turning to coat top, cover with plastic wrap, and let rise until doubled, about 1 hour.

Turn out onto a lightly floured surface, and divide in half. Pat each half into a rectangle, and then fold in thirds, like folding a business letter. Pinch seam closed, and roll to make a baguette shape. Place on a greased baking sheet lightly dusted with cornmeal. Make several slashes with a sharp knife across top of each loaf. Cover with a cloth, and let rise until doubled, about 1 hour.

CHAR'S BAKING TIPS

• Keep trying; it's never the same each time you bake.

• I enjoy making bread with my little grandkids. I just give them a small ball of dough, and it's fun to see what they make.

• My mother-in-law never measured any ingredients, which taught me to pay more attention to how the dough feels. Dough can behave differently from one season to the next, depending on temperature and humidity, so it's better to adjust your ingredients than to strictly follow measurements.

• Let your bread rise in your microwave oven. Some have an oven light that provides enough warmth.

Preheat oven to 350° F.

Arrange oven racks so that you can put an empty cake pan on lowest rack and bread on middle rack. Place in oven. Carefully, pour 1 cup hot water into cake pan. Quickly, close oven door, and bake for 25 minutes. Remove loaves, brush with 1 beaten egg white, and then return to oven for 5 to 10 minutes. Cool on wire rack.

Whole Wheat Bread

This recipe for a light and tender whole wheat loaf is one Char learned from her mother-in-law. It started her on a lifetime of bread baking.

MAKES 2 LOAVES.

1	tablespoon active dry yeast
½	cup warm water
2	cups water
⅓	cup honey
1	tablespoon salt
¼	cup vegetable oil
2	cups whole wheat flour
2½	to 3 cups all-purpose flour

In a large bowl dissolve yeast in ½ cup water, and let sit until foamy, about 5 minutes. Add 2 cups water, honey, salt, oil, and whole wheat flour; mix well. Gradually, add all-purpose flour until dough forms a kneadable mass. Turn out onto a lightly floured surface, and knead 5 to 10 minutes, adding as little flour as possible. Place in an oiled bowl, turning to coat top, cover with plastic wrap, and let rise until doubled, about 1 hour.

Turn out onto a lightly floured surface, kneading to deflate, and divide in half. Shape into loaves, and place in greased bread pans. Cover with a cloth, and let rise until doubled, about 45 minutes.

Preheat oven to 350° F.

Bake for 30 to 35 minutes or until loaves sound hollow when tapped on bottom. Remove bread from pans, and cool on wire racks.

Dilly Bread

This recipe came from one of Char's favorite aunts. If you can make it in the summer with fresh dill weed, boost the amount to four teaspoons of herb, finely chopped. **MAKES 1 ROUND LOAF.**

1 tablespoon active dry yeast
¼ cup warm water
1 cup small-curd cottage cheese
1 tablespoon butter, salted or unsalted
2 teaspoons dried dill weed or 4 teaspoons fresh dill weed
1 tablespoon minced onion
1 teaspoon salt
1 large egg
2½ to 3 cups all-purpose flour

In a large bowl dissolve yeast in warm water, and set aside until foamy, about 5 minutes. Meanwhile, in a saucepan over low heat, gently warm cottage cheese and butter, and then add to yeast, along with dill, onion, salt, and egg. Mix well. Add flour, and mix well. Turn out onto a lightly floured surface, and knead several minutes. Place in an oiled bowl, turning to coat top, cover with plastic wrap, and let rise until doubled, about 1 hour.

Preheat oven to 350° F.

Turn out, knead slightly, shape, and then place in a greased casserole dish or a pie pan. Cover with a cloth, and let rise until doubled, about 30 minutes. Bake for 30 to 35 minutes. Cool on a wire rack.

CHAR'S RECOMMENDED READING

• *Sunset Book of Breads* (Menlo Park, CA: Sunset Books, 1966). This book is my favorite bread book. It is now available in a new edition: Sunset publishing staff, *Breads*, 5th ed. (1994).

• Congregation of Our Savior's Lutheran Church, *Our Savior's Lutheran Church Cook Book* (Kiester, MN). I've had this for 50 years.

• Betty Crocker, *Make It Now, Serve It Later: Refrigerator Recipes from Betty Crocker* (Minneapolis, MN: General Mills, 1984).

• Charlotte Turgeon, *The Encyclopedia of Creative Cooking* (New York: Crown Publishing, 1985).

Will Powers

HIS WORLD OF BREAD

The Law, in its majestic equality, forbids the rich, as well as the poor, to sleep under bridges, to beg in the streets, and to steal bread.

ANATOLE FRANCE

So, the story goes that the phone rang and it was Will Powers's wife calling home from her family's cabin at the Lake of the Woods, where he was about to drive to join her and some relatives for a summer vacation. Please, she said, bake some bread before you leave. There's nothing worth slicing up here. Love ya, bye!

Or something to that effect. The trouble was, there wasn't really time to bake bread from start to finish. At one point in Will's life, this would have been a problem. Now, though, it loomed as an opportunity to experiment. He made the dough, tightly covered the huge bowl, nestled it in the trunk of his car, and headed north.

"That dough must have wondered what was happening at some points," he said, recalling a particularly pioneering stretch of gravel road. Thankfully, Canadian customs officials never opened his trunk, although that only would have made the story better. In any case, the dough arrived, nicely risen. Shaped and baked, it fortified them through their vacation.

Will, sixty-one, told the story by way of demonstrating the incredible resiliency of bread dough and how it adjusts to setbacks. The trouble is, sometimes its most formidable setback is us.

When Will began making bread, he focused on precise measurements, both of ingredients and of time. "I followed the directions to let the dough rise for 1½ hours, and I'd set the clock," he said. "I don't know why my eyes never saw the phrase 'or until doubled,' but I'd set that timer for 1½ hours, and that was it. Boy, I made some doorstops."

That changed one winter evening when he was planning a dinner party for the following night. He wanted fresh bread but would be up against the clock the next day. "So I started the dough late and set it to rise in the cool kitchen around midnight." He awoke the next morning to dough that had finally gotten the chance to slowly rise until it had doubled in bulk. The resulting loaf was marvelous. "The scales fell from my eyes."

Now, he said, his bread baking provokes less worry and actually gives him more time. "Now I'll make the dough and then go for a walk or run some errands. And if I run into a friend and we go to a bar for a while, it's OK, it'll just rise more. I don't think I've baked an overproofed loaf yet."

It's a little ironic, maybe, that Will began baking bread to kill time. In 1968 when he was starting out as a typographer in Ohio, his boss made a practice of giving a copy of *The World of Bread* to nice young couples just starting out. Will doesn't think the guy ever actually baked bread, "but he and his wife were sort of protohippies, and I think they thought this was a way to make a community."

But the book sat unopened until a few years later when Will moved to northern Vermont, to a town of boring bread and few diversions. The book became a source of both recreation and sustenance. "Every week of my life since then, I've baked bread," he said.

Oh wait, except for those years in the mid-1980s when he lived in Berkeley, California, just down the road from the Acme Bread Company, a bakery founded a few years earlier by Steve Sullivan and widely considered the birthplace of the artisanal bread movement. "I thought, why compete?"

Then, in 1990 Will and Cheryl Miller moved to Birchwood, near White Bear Lake. As a book designer, he's kept an eye on the publishing world and is amazed at the explosion in books about bread. The foundation laid by the folks at Acme finally has permeated the national consciousness.

He reserves his baking budget for equipment, which he essentially, and frugally, sums up as a great big bowl. His is stainless steel and big enough for several loaves' worth of dough. "It's great for being able to make big moves with your spoon and your arms," he said. "And you can do your initial kneading in the bowl, which holds down the mess."

A big bowl also gives him a better view of the dough, especially important after he had a breakthrough about adding flour. Instead of dumping in what the recipe calls for all at once, he adds it a flour scoop at a time and then eventually just a handful at a time until it looks and feels right.

His other equipment is the stuff of daily life. He likes to bake bread in unusual shapes—a Pyrex saucepan, a clay flowerpot, or a tin can. Cheryl came through with the brainstorm of giving a particularly recalcitrant flatbread dough a run through the pasta maker. In other words, bread is a vehicle for the imagination.

"I think we all have a creative need," Will said. "I don't make anything else because I don't really need much, and there's not room here for much. So bread is perfect for someone who needs to make something, but something that doesn't take up any space. I mean, I make it, and in a few days, it's gone."

Winter Midnight Bulgur Bread

Will said he's been working on this recipe for about twenty years and is "finally satisfied with it." It incorporates a basic recipe for cracked wheat bread from The World of Breads *by Dolores Casella and one for* pane integrale *from* More Classic Italian Cooking *by Marcella Hazan. Baking this bread in a Pullman pan, with its sliding lid, results in the ideal sandwich shape with a crust all around of deep mahogany. This bread makes use of highly seasoned sesame oil. Will says that a few drops is all you need. (Store it in the refrigerator; it easily goes rancid.)* **MAKES 2 TO 3 LOAVES, DEPENDING ON SIZE AND SHAPE.** *And no, you don't have to wait until midnight to make it.*

2 cups bulgur
4 cups very hot water
3 tablespoons olive oil
A few drops roasted sesame oil
6 teaspoons salt
3 tablespoons active dry yeast
6 cups all-purpose flour, about

Shortly before midnight (or thereabouts) pour hot water over bulgur. Add salt and oils, and let cool to lukewarm. Add yeast, and let sit awhile. Gradually, add and mix in flour until dough is stiff enough to knead by hand.

Knead about 10 minutes, place in an oiled bowl, turning to coat top, cover with plastic wrap, and place in a cool room. Take a walk, see the stars, and then go to bed.

In the morning the dough should be risen when you rise. Punch down, cover with a towel, and let rise a few more hours in a cool place until doubled. Turn out onto a lightly floured surface, and shape into loaves. Will likes to make a flat round loaf, about ½ inch thick, to bake on a pizza stone; a couple of submarine-shaped rolls; and maybe a sandwich loaf for his lidded Pullman pan. Cover and let rise again until doubled, about 45 minutes.

Preheat oven to 450° F.

Bake for 12 minutes. Reduce heat to 375° F, and bake up to 40 minutes more for large loaves, less for smaller loaves. Bread should sound hollow when thumped on bottom. Cool on a wire rack.

WILL'S BAKING TIPS

• Clean bowls and tools after each step. Few substances are as pernicious as flour and water left too long. Don't use a dishwasher. Wash them in the sink, and look out the window at the birds in your yard.

• If you or the people you bake for eat sandwiches, get a Pullman pan (online and at specialty stores). The loaves are nearly square and are very dense. Depending on your recipe, you can get a thick, even crust all around.

• Bulk, not time, is the factor that determines if a dough has risen enough. Do not be a slave to the clock. Remember Marcella Hazan's thought about the possibility that bread dough may rise too much: "It has nowhere else to go."

• The first goal is to get to the point where you can know your dough by feel, not by how closely you have followed a recipe. The second goal is to understand how far you can stray while experimenting. Experiment often.

• Early on, if you make a loaf that better resembles a doorstop, actually use it as a doorstop for a while. It will be a daily object lesson—and an encouragement.

Chipotle Anadama Bread

"This recipe is based on Anadama Bread in The World of Breads *by Dolores Casella. I cannot recall the origin of my version, other than my constant desire for hot food. I took the molasses out of the original in favor of the chipotles and substituted bacon fat for the butter. Be careful of how much chipotle peppers and sauce you use; start slowly if spicy food is not your usual fare."* **MAKES 2 LOAVES.**

- 2 cups water
- ½ cup bacon fat, or unsalted butter
- 2 cups whole milk, scalded
- 2 cups traditional polenta
- ⅓ cup (½ 7-ounce can) chipotle peppers in adobo sauce, finely chopped
- 4 teaspoons salt
- 3 tablespoons active dry yeast
- 7 to 8 cups all-purpose flour

Combine water and bacon fat in saucepan, and bring to a boil to melt fat. Add scalded milk, and pour over polenta in a large bowl. Add chipotles and salt, mix well, and let cool to lukewarm. Stir in yeast, and let sit, about 5 to 10 minutes.

Gradually, add flour, 1 cup at a time, stirring until dough is firm enough to be kneaded. Knead for several minutes, then place in an oiled bowl, turning to coat top. Cover with plastic wrap, and let rise until doubled, about 1 hour.

Turn out onto a lightly floured surface, shape into 2 loaves, and place in buttered loaf pans. Cover with a cloth, and let rise until doubled.

Preheat oven to 375° F.

Bake for about 45 minutes or until loaves sound hollow when thumped on bottom. Remove from pans, and cool on a rack.

Garlic and Cheese Fougasse

Gino's Kitchen *by Gino Dalesandro (1997) is the starting place for this fougasse (foo-GAHS) recipe. Gino wanted his readers to roll the dough into cigar-like pieces and then twist them into what he calls "garlic knots." "These are fantastic," Will said, "but sometimes that's just too much work, so I came up with a way to incorporate the oil, garlic, and cheese into the body of the loaf. Then I simply roll out the dough into a couple of full moon fougasse loaves and bake them that way."* **MAKES 2 OR 3 LOAVES.**

3 tablespoons active dry yeast
3 cups lukewarm water
4 tablespoons extra-virgin olive oil, divided
3 or 4 garlic cloves, depending on your taste for garlic
6 teaspoons salt
9 cups bread flour
⅓ cup grated Parmesan cheese
Coarse black pepper (optional)

Mix yeast and water in large bowl; set aside. Slice garlic cloves very thinly and simmer in small saucepan with 3 tablespoons of the olive oil until garlic is soft. Watch carefully; if garlic browns, it will turn bitter. Remove garlic from saucepan and smash with a mortar and pestle until a paste has formed. Return garlic to oil.

Add 3 cups flour and all the salt to yeast and water. Thoroughly mix in half the cheese and half the oil and garlic. When the dough is smooth, thoroughly mix in 3 more cups of flour, the remaining oil and garlic, and the rest of the cheese. Add two more cups of flour and mix until the dough is smooth. Now mix in remaining cup of flour a bit at a time until you have a smooth, firm dough. Let rise until doubled. Punch down and let rise until doubled again.

Preheat oven to 400° F, with pizza stones in place.

While the oven is getting up to heat, shape 2 or 3 *fougasse* loaves by hand and with a rolling pin. They may be as large as you like, but no more than ⅓-inch thick.

Place each loaf on a peel that you have covered with polenta (coarse corn meal). Brush remaining tablespoon of oil on tops of loaves. If you want to add coarse pepper for more zing, tap loaves all over with the tines of a fork, forming small indentations, then brush with olive oil and sprinkle with pepper.

Slide loaves onto heated pizza stones and bake about 30 minutes. The tops of the loaves should have small bubbles and the tops of the bubbles should have started to brown. If this is the case, remove from oven and cool on a rack.

Breadcrumb Muffins

"We cut leftover bread into chunks and dump them into a bowl with a piece of cooking parchment loosely laid on top. This bowl sits atop the kitchen cabinets until we need croutons or breadcrumbs. In time they are wonderfully hard, and for some reason they do not get moldy. When I need crumbs, I put a handful into my big mortar and wham them with the pestle. Among their end uses is this old-time recipe." **MAKES 9 MUFFINS.**

- 1 cup crumbs from dry bread, pounded by hand or pulsed in a blender
- 1 cup lowfat milk
- 1 large egg
- 1 cup all-purpose flour
- 1 tablespoon sugar
- ½ teaspoon salt
- 1 tablespoon baking powder
- ¼ cup unsalted butter, melted

Preheat oven to 375° F.

In a medium bowl mix crumbs, milk, and egg. In another bowl mix dry ingredients, and then stir into crumb mixture. Add melted butter. Mix until all dry ingredients are completely moist, but do not overdo it. Put mixture in buttered muffin tins, filling each cup about two-thirds full.

Bake for 25 to 30 minutes. Serve warm.

Karen Vogl

A COMPETITIVE ZEAL

Things to be observed in the well making of Bread—whereof we must have great choices and care: 1) of the Wheate itself, 2) of the Meal, 3) of the Water, 4) of the Salt, 5) of the Leaven, 6) of the Dough or Past, 7) of the Moulding, 8) of the Oven, 9) of the Baking. All which circumstances I most willingly prosecute to the full, because as Bread is the best nourishment of all other, being well made, so it is simply the worst being marred in the ill handling.

THOMAS MUFFETT, *Health's Improvement,* **1595**

Karen Vogl leaned forward across her kitchen table in confidence and then drew back, as if some inner contest was being waged. Turns out there often is, as became clear when she decided to spill the beans. "I'm a competitive person," she said and then smiled, "although I hate to admit that about myself." As with most people who are serious about their craft, she is her chief competitor.

Sometimes, she's competing with the Karen who made that burnished *boule* of peasant bread last week. Other times, it's the Karen who tackled the floury *ciabatta* last month. "But I'm also competing against the bread you get in a nice restaurant," she said, and the amazing breads she remembers from living in Germany many years ago.

Her competitive zeal occasionally brings the oven repairman to her house, especially when her opponent is the Karen who seeks the perfect baguette. "I'm consumed with the idea of finding a recipe that works," she said. "I'm going to get a baguette that has the right texture, the holes, the crust." All of which brings us to the pan of rocks on the floor of her oven.

A great baguette has a crust like no other bread. It's a caramelized sheath of parchment's heft, yet it shatters with a satisfying snap, like the ice of a winter puddle cracking underfoot in the woodland near her home in North Oaks. To get that sound, you need steam.

Her pursuit is not for the fainthearted. Everyone has a theory, often accompanied by a cautionary tale. Some say to spritz the bread with a spray bottle of water as you place it in the oven—although the oven's light bulb may burst if it gets wet. Or fill a pan with boiling water as you load your bread—but don't lose any oven heat while you're doing it. Or throw a handful of ice cubes on the oven floor. Or bake enough loaves at once so that they create their own steam.

Or turn your oven into a sauna with a pan of rocks and some water. This theory is Karen's. Here's her cautionary tale:

"I've bent the floor of my oven by putting in too many rocks, and the steam has made the power cut out," Karen said. She tried to appear sheepish, but any humility is canceled out by the knowledge that she makes a great baguette—almost all of the time.

It's the "almost" thing that either makes a baker go crazy or get better. A better baker knows how flour changes with Minnesota's seasons—dry as a chapped cheek in the winter or invisibly sodden with humidity in the summer.

Her touchstone is a recipe for cinnamon rolls. "I've made cinnamon rolls my whole life," she said. She branched out to make her aunt's rye bread, but to little acclaim on the home front. "My kids, who are now in their thirties, were embarrassed by having homemade bread in their school lunches."

Her baking tapered off. Then about eight years ago, a friend gave her Joe Ortiz's *The Village Baker* for Christmas, and she set out to bake her way through it. For Karen, sixty-eight, baking is a change of pace, a welcome shift from the number crunching she does for a living. "I look at it as a hobby or craft, like making a quilt or throwing pots. But you can only do so many of those. I mean, people don't usually need one more quilt or one more pot. But everyone always needs bread. It's fun to give away. You feel good, and they feel good, and it gives you an excuse to make some more."

Cinnamon Rolls

Karen gives away dozens of these during the holidays. **MAKES 6 ROLLS LARGE ENOUGH TO INSPIRE SHARING WITH A FRIEND OVER COFFEE OR 2 WREATHS.** *This dough without the cinnamon filling also can be used to make plain dinner rolls of any shape.*

Dough

  2 large eggs

1½ cups warm water

  1 tablespoon active dry yeast

  ½ cup nonfat dry milk

  ¼ cup sugar

  ¼ cup canola oil

4½ cups all-purpose flour, about

1½ teaspoons salt

Filling

  3 tablespoons unsalted butter, melted

  ½ cup light brown sugar, packed

  2 teaspoons cinnamon

In a large mixing bowl beat eggs. Add water, yeast, dry milk, sugar, and oil, and mix well. Add 3 cups flour, and mix well. Mix in salt. Add 1 more cup flour. Knead with a mixer that has a dough hook attachment or by hand, adding additional flour as needed. Place in an oiled bowl, turning to coat top. Cover with plastic wrap, and let rise until doubled, about 1 to 2 hours.

Turn out onto a lightly floured surface, and roll into a 28-by-12-inch rectangle. Brush with melted butter. Combine brown sugar with cinnamon, and sprinkle evenly over dough. From widest side, roll up like a jellyroll.

For rolls cut the 28-inch cylinder into 5 or 6 logs, each about 5 to 6 inches long. For wreaths cut 28-inch cylinder in half, and shape into 2 circles, pinching ends together. Place on a cookie sheet covered with parchment paper. Cut slashes every 1 to 2 inches for expansion and decoration for both rolls and wreaths. Cover with a cloth, and let rise until doubled, about 1 hour.

Preheat oven to 350° F.

Bake for 25 to 27 minutes. Cool on rack.

Frost with a powdered sugar glaze or frosting of 2 tablespoons butter, 1 teaspoon vanilla, 1 cup powdered sugar, and enough milk to make a spreadable consistency.

Baguette

This bread inspired one of Karen's most treasured reactions. "I have a friend who is a real food snob. I still remember her commenting about the good bread and the surprised look on her face when someone else told her that I had baked the baguette." Karen likes to use an organic flour with wheat germ from Swany White Flour Mills in Freeport, Minnesota.

MAKES 4 LARGE OR 8 SMALL BAGUETTES.

Sponge

    2   cups unbleached white organic flour
    1   package active dry yeast
    1½ cups warm water

Dough

    1½ cups warm water
    1   teaspoon active dry yeast
    5   to 6 cups unbleached white organic flour
    1   tablespoon salt

For sponge, in a medium bowl combine 2 cups flour, 1 package yeast, and warm water, and mix well. Cover with plastic wrap, and let rise in a warm place for 8 hours or overnight. The sponge mixture will rise and fall during that time.

In a large bowl combine sponge mixture with water and yeast. Mix well, and then gradually add flour. After almost all flour has been added, add salt, and mix well. This dough is very moist, which helps make those big holes so prized in baguettes.

Knead by mixer or by hand, about 10 to 15 minutes. On a lightly floured surface, cut into desired number of pieces, and shape into baguettes. Place on parchment-covered baking sheets, cover with a cloth, and let rise until doubled, about 45 minutes. Preheat oven to 500° F. If you have a baking stone, preheat for 30 minutes.

Make several slashes on top of each loaf. Bake for 15 to 18 minutes. If using a baking stone, slide parchment paper with loaves onto stone.

For a crisper crust spray loaves with water just before placing in oven, or put a pan of boiling water on the lowest shelf. Karen heats a pan filled with sauna rocks and then pours ½ to 1 cup of water over the rocks when she puts the bread in the oven.

Irish Soda Bread

Some soda breads have gotten progressively softer and sweeter with each generation. Not this one. Here is a loaf of the Auld Sod. Karen likes to press some additional oatmeal onto the top of the loaf before cutting the traditional X on the top. **MAKES 1 LARGE LOAF.**

3	cups whole wheat flour
1	cup all-purpose flour
½	cup old-fashioned oatmeal
¼	teaspoon salt
1	teaspoon baking soda
2	large eggs
2	cups buttermilk

Preheat oven to 375° F. In a medium bowl mix whole wheat and all-purpose flour, oatmeal, salt, and soda. In a small bowl mix together eggs and buttermilk. Add to flour mixture, and mix well. This dough will be very heavy. Turn out onto a lightly floured surface, and knead just to make sure that all flour is moistened. Shape into a round, and place on a greased baking sheet. Press additional oatmeal into top. With a sharp knife slash an X across loaf. Bake for 40 to 50 minutes.

Aunt Anna's Swedish Rye Bread

This recipe is sweetened with sorghum, a light style of molasses made from the stalks of the sorghum plant, which is a cereal grain, rather than from the sugar cane of regular molasses. Scented with a heady combination of spices, this bread has traveled through the generations. **MAKES 2 LOAVES.**

1½ cups rye flour
¾ teaspoon salt
¼ cup packed brown sugar
¼ cup sorghum
2 tablespoons molasses
2 tablespoons honey
1 tablespoon canola oil
2 cups hot water
½ teaspoon mixed spices (anise, fennel, and caraway seeds ground together)
1 package active dry yeast
¼ cup warm water
½ teaspoon sugar
4 to 4 ½ cups all-purpose flour

In a medium bowl combine rye flour, salt, brown sugar, sorghum, molasses, honey, and oil, and then pour in hot water. Mix well, and let cool. Add spices.

In a large bowl sprinkle yeast over warm water. Add sugar, and let yeast stand until foamy, about 5 minutes. Stir into rye flour mixture. Add all-purpose flour 1 cup at a time, mixing thoroughly. Turn out onto a lightly floured surface, and knead until dough is resilient and no longer sticky, about 10 to 15 minutes. Place in an oiled bowl, turning to coat top, cover with plastic wrap, and let rise until doubled, about 1 to 2 hours.

Punch down, turn out onto board, and shape into 2 loaves. Place in greased pans, cover with a cloth, and let rise until doubled, about 45 minutes.

Preheat oven to 350° F.

Bake for 45 minutes or until bread sounds hollow when thumped on bottom. Remove from pans, and cool on a wire rack.

Country Peasant Bread

Karen sometimes varies the proportions of white, whole wheat, and cracked wheat flours, just making sure that they total 5 to 5½ cups. This loaf bakes to a deep burnished brown. **MAKES 8 SMALL OR 4 LARGE LOAVES.**

Sponge
- 1 cup all-purpose flour
- ½ cup whole wheat flour
- ½ cup rye flour
- 1 package active dry yeast
- 1½ cups warm water

Dough
- 1½ cups warm water
- 1½ teaspoons active dry yeast
- 1 cup cracked wheat flour
- 2 cups whole wheat flour
- 2 to 2½ cups all-purpose flour
- 1 tablespoon salt

For sponge, combine all-purpose, whole wheat, and rye flours; yeast; and warm water, and mix thoroughly. Cover with plastic wrap, and let rise in a warm place for at least 8 hours or overnight. The mixture will rise and fall.

Dissolve yeast in warm water, and add to sponge. Stir in wheat flours and salt. Gradually, add all-purpose flour, and knead by hand or by mixer, about 10 minutes. Shape into the size loaves you prefer, and place on baking sheets lightly dusted with cornmeal. Cover with a cloth, and let rise until doubled, about 1 hour.

Preheat oven to 450° F.

Slash loaves decoratively, place in oven, and then reduce heat to 400° F. Bake for 30 to 35 minutes or until loaves sound hollow when tapped on bottom.

For a crisper crust spray loaves with water just before placing in oven, or put a pan of boiling water on the lowest shelf. Karen likes to bake the bread on baking tiles or a pizza stone that has been thoroughly heated.

Rosemary Focaccia with Olives

This recipe originally called for using a food processor, but you retain more control over your dough by mixing with a stand mixer or with your hands. It's adapted from a recipe in the September 1999 issue of Bon Appétit.

MAKES 1 THIRTEEN-INCH ROUND BREAD.

1	12- to 16-ounce russet potato (or ⅔ cup instant potato flakes dissolved in ⅔ cup warm water)
2½	cups (or more) bread flour
3	teaspoons fresh rosemary leaves, chopped
1	teaspoon salt
1	cup warm water
¼	teaspoon sugar
1	package active dry yeast
4	tablespoons extra-virgin olive oil
12	oil-cured black olives, pitted and halved
½	teaspoon coarse sea salt

Pierce potato several times with a fork, and microwave on high until tender, turning once, about 12 minutes. Let cool slightly, and cut in half. Scoop flesh into small bowl, and mash well. Measure ⅔ cup packed mashed potato; cool. (Reserve extra potato for another use, or just get out the butter and salt and have a snack right now.)

In a medium bowl combine 2½ cups flour, half the rosemary, and 1 teaspoon salt. Add potato, and mix to blend. In a small bowl combine warm water, sugar, and yeast, and let stand until foamy, about 5 minutes. Stir in 3 table-spoons oil.

Pour yeast mixture into flour, and mix until smooth, about 1 minute. Scrape dough onto a lightly floured surface, and knead until silky, sprinkling more flour as needed. The gluten in focaccia dough should not be developed, so knead for 1 minute or less. Place in a large oiled bowl, turning to coat top, cover with plastic wrap, and let rise until doubled, about 1 hour.

Position rack in center of oven, and preheat to 450° F.

Brush a large baking sheet with oil. Punch down dough, and knead for 30 seconds on a lightly floured surface. Stretch or pat dough to a 12-inch round. Transfer round to baking sheet, and press all over with fingertips to make dimples. Brush with 1 tablespoon oil. Press olive halves, cut side down, into dough. Sprinkle with sea salt. Cover with a cloth, and let rise until just puffy, about 20 minutes. Bake until golden, about 18 minutes.

KAREN'S BAKING TIPS

• I am not very successful in telling whether I have kneaded enough, so I let most breads rise in a large plastic container with a lid on it. If after fifteen to twenty minutes the dough spreads more than it rises, fold the sides over to the center to form a ball, and flip it over so the smooth side is on top. Do this every fifteen to twenty minutes, three or four times total. It helps develop the bread's structure, and after the third or fourth time, the dough rises instead of only expanding horizontally.

• I use what looks like an oversized salt shaker from a restaurant supply store to spread a thin layer of flour evenly on a work surface without getting clumps.

• Depending on the humidity of where it has been stored, flour absorbs different amounts of water. It is not unusual for the amount of flour used in a recipe to vary by as much as half of a cup from time to time. Pay more attention to the dough than to the measuring cup.

• Many bread recipes calling for milk require it first to be scalded by warming in a saucepan until small bubbles begin to appear around the edge. Heating the milk changes its proteins, destroying enzymes to better affect how it performs in the recipe. Plus, warmed milk helps encourage the growth of the yeast. Scalding can be futzy, however, so instead, to save a step and a dirty pan, Karen always uses powdered milk and warm water combined in the correct proportions.

David Cargo

BUILDING COMMUNITY THROUGH BREAD

So I was having a good enough time seeing them hunt for my remainders if I only had a bite to eat. Well, then I happened to think how they always put quicksilver in loaves of bread and float them off, because they always go right to the drownded carcass and stop there. So, says I, I'll keep a lookout . . . by and by along comes another one, and this time I won. I took out the plug and shook out the little dab of quicksilver, and set my teeth in. It was "baker's bread"—what the quality eat; none of your low-down corn-pone.

MARK TWAIN, The Adventures of Huckleberry Finn

David Cargo goes by "David S. Cargo," which means he gets to have license plates that read "ESCARGO" Pretty cool. Nevertheless, he has embraced the harvest of the land as a vegetarian for twenty-seven years and as a home baker in college. Long ago, his heart was won by the freshness of home-baked bread. "Even a loaf of frozen Rhodes dough that's right out of the oven, spread with honey and butter, is just ambrosia."

David is almost as passionate about the bread club. He is its webmaster and vice president of communications, and an instigator of monthly chat sessions at local coffeehouses such as Sisu Coffee and Café in St. Paul and another at the Eden Prairie Mall for more westerly members. His dream is to convince the city of St. Paul of the need for a wood-fired brick bread oven in a park where citizens can gather for communal bakes, just as their ancestors might have done in their various homelands.

"The bread club definitely is one of the things that gives us an opportunity to build community," he said. "Clearly, there is a lot of enthusiasm."

He also may be the only member with a claim to having made a living at baking when he was between jobs as a computer engineer a few years ago. He manned the ovens at Trotter's Café and Bakery, the family-owned restaurant near his Highland Park neighborhood, before returning to a higher-tech world.

So it's back to bytes, but he'll always bake. He has grown increasingly focused on his breads over the past several years, partly motivated by health issues. He has developed diabetes and said, "I realized if I did my own baking, I would know what was in the food I was eating, better than going to the store."

For four years, David also has been part of a ten-year longitudinal study by the University of Minnesota into how people maintain weight loss. From a high of 246 pounds, he's now lean as a baguette and keeps a meticulous log of everything he eats. He weighs every portion. Every day. For years.

OK, so we have a guy whose life is in many ways defined by boundaries, analysis, and high technology. So it comes as a surprise, and a delight, that he refers to his culinary philosophy as a serendipitous "Baking with Leftovers."

David's breads morph and change depending upon what's in which container in his refrigerator. Maybe it's some squash from last night or wild rice from Sunday's supper. A dollop of cottage cheese and a bunch of scallions results in cottage cheese–onion bread. Grate the peel from that last orange, use up the rest of the cranberries, and he's got a lovely quick bread. A last swipe of mayonnaise adds tang.

"Bread is such a versatile food that just about any ingredient can be incorporated into it," he said. "So if I have shallots, olives, mushrooms, and ricotta cheese that I need to use, I can make a great savory bread using all of them. Once you have a good base dough that you know you can work with, you can vary it."

Often, though, he makes his baking choices by considering what flour he has on hand at the moment. "If you can't remember how many kinds of flour you have, you're a good baker."

Milk Bread

Klecko calls this David's "mother dough," and it provides the basis for a wide variety of breads. It makes an excellent sandwich loaf with a fine crumb yet is quite sturdy and toasts well. While this is a milk bread, David prefers half-and-half for the most tender results. Then again, it depends on what he has in the fridge. **MAKES 1 LOAF.**

1¼ cups half-and-half, or milk
1 teaspoon sugar
1 package active dry yeast
3½ cups bread flour
1 teaspoon salt

Heat half-and-half over low heat to lukewarm. Pour into mixing bowl, and add sugar and yeast. Wait 5 minutes for yeast to foam.

Add 2 cups flour and salt, and mix thoroughly. Add more flour until a smooth dough forms. If necessary, dribble in water until dough comes together. Knead for 10 minutes or until smooth and springy. Place in an oiled bowl, turning to coat top, cover with plastic wrap, and let rise until doubled, about 1 hour.

Punch down dough, and turn out onto a lightly floured surface. Press gently into an oval or rectangle, fold in long sides, and pinch together to form a smooth cylinder. Place seam side down in a buttered bread pan, cover with a cloth, and put in a warm place to rise until doubled, about 1 hour.

Preheat oven to 375° F.

Bake for 30 minutes or until loaf sounds hollow when thumped on bottom. Remove from pan, and cool on wire rack.

Bun Variation

Mix the recipe as usual, but add about ⅓ cup finely chopped shallots. After the first rise divide dough into 10 to 12 portions, and form into bun shapes, flattening while placing on 2 baking sheets lined with parchment paper. Cover with a cloth, and let rise until doubled, about 45 minutes.

Preheat oven to 400° F.

Bake for 20 minutes. Rotate pans after 10 minutes to ensure even browning.

Jalapeño Breadsticks

Green nuggets of fresh jalapeño make these especially attractive, and baking eases the heat to piquant levels. David said these inspired the most treasured reaction he's ever received: "My grandson smacked his lips when someone mentioned my jalapeño breadsticks." **MAKES ABOUT 32 BREADSTICKS.**

1	tablespoon extra-virgin olive oil
1	medium onion, finely chopped
1¼	cups 2% milk
1	package active dry yeast
1½	teaspoons sugar
1½	teaspoons salt
3	ounces jalapeño peppers, seeded and coarsely chopped
3¾	cups bread flour
	Choice of pretzel salt, herbs, or shredded cheese (Parmesan or Jack are nice) for topping

Sauté onions in olive oil until just translucent. Set aside. Heat milk over low heat to lukewarm, pour into mixing bowl, and then add sugar and yeast. Set aside until yeast foams, about 5 minutes. Add 1 cup flour and salt, and mix to a moist dough. Add enough remaining flour to make a workable dough. (If your flour needs more moisture, slowly dribble in water until dough comes together.) Mix in onions and chopped jalapeños. Knead by hand for 10 minutes or with a mixer and a dough hook until dough is springy. (In a mixer dough will cleanly pull away from sides of bowl when done.) Let rest for 10 minutes.

Preheat oven to 400° F.

Turn out onto a lightly floured surface, and divide into 30 to 32 pieces. Roll out into breadstick shapes about 8 inches long. Place on lightly greased baking sheets, cover with a cloth, and let rise until puffy, about 20 minutes. Brush tops with water or milk, and sprinkle with pretzel salt, herbs, or shredded cheese. Bake for 20 minutes or until golden brown.

Garlic Pull-apart Bread

When sautéing garlic, watch it carefully, heating it just until plump. "If you sauté it too long, you will get a sticky mess, and you will need to start over with new butter, garlic, and probably a different pan." This loaf is great for setting on the table and letting guests peel off a piece at a time. It was a blue-ribbon winner in the club's 2004 bake-off. **MAKES 1 LOAF.**

1	cup half-and-half
1	tablespoon sugar
1	package active dry yeast
1	teaspoon salt
2½	cups bread flour
2	tablespoons unsalted butter
6	to 8 cloves garlic, minced or pressed

Warm half-and-half over low heat to lukewarm. Pour into mixing bowl, add sugar and yeast, and let sit until yeast foams, about 5 minutes. Add 1 cup flour and salt, and mix to a moist dough. Add remaining flour, and mix until a workable dough results, adding some water if necessary. Knead by hand for 10 minutes or with a dough hook until dough cleanly pulls away from sides of bowl. Let rest for 10 minutes.

In the meantime briefly sauté garlic in butter, and then set aside. On a lightly floured surface roll dough into an 8-by-12-inch rectangle. Spread garlic and butter mixture over rectangle all the way to edges. Slice rectangle into four 3-by-8-inch strips. Stack strips, and slice crosswise into four 3-by-2-inch rectangles. Take stacks, and put into a buttered 8½-by-4½-by-2-inch loaf pan, arranged cut edge down. The arrangement will look kind of like an accordion pleat. Cover with a cloth, and let rise in a warm place until slices fill pan, about 1 hour.

Preheat oven to 375° F.

Bake for about 30 minutes or until golden brown. Immediately invert bread onto a wire cooling rack with a sheet pan beneath to catch bits of garlic that fall off. This is best eaten warm, but may also be reheated.

For a sweet variation substitute garlic with 1 tablespoon soft butter spread on rectangle, and then sprinkle with ¼ cup brown sugar and 1 tablespoon cinnamon. Continue as directed.

Snail Rolls

This shape of breakfast treat is an unusual variation from the traditional wreath or rosette of sweet rolls. But then not many of us have the inspiration of escargot. This bread took third place in the "sweet dough" category in 2005.

Dough
1½	cups 2% milk
1	package active dry yeast
¼	cup sugar
1	tablespoon cinnamon
1	teaspoon salt
1	large egg, beaten
3½	cups bread flour

Filling

　1　tablespoon unsalted butter, softened
　¼　cup dark brown sugar
　1　tablespoon ground cinnamon
　½　teaspoon nutmeg

Icing

　1　cup powdered sugar, sifted
　1　teaspoon vanilla extract
　2　teaspoons 2% milk

Heat milk over low heat to lukewarm, and pour into a mixing bowl. Mix in yeast and 1 tablespoon sugar, and wait for mixture to foam, about 5 minutes. Add remaining sugar, cinnamon, salt, egg, and 2 cups flour, and mix until combined. Add remaining flour ¼ cup at a time until a smooth dough pulls away from walls of mixing bowl. Dough should be soft but not sticky. Knead with dough hook for 8 minutes, dusting with flour if needed to keep from sticking to bowl.

On a lightly floured surface, roll out into a 10-by-16-inch rectangle. Spread butter to within ½ inch of top edge. Mix brown sugar and spices, and sprinkle evenly over buttered surface. Roll up from one long side, and seal top seam. Turn seam side down.

Cover a large baking sheet with baking parchment. Transfer roll to baking sheet. Using a sharp knife, make cuts 1 inch apart, cutting three-quarters of the way through the roll.

Carefully, center one end of roll on baking sheet, and twist first piece of centered end until lying flat. Pick up and move roll clockwise around first piece, and twist next piece until it lies flat. Repeat with each piece in turn, creating a spiral. Cover with a cloth, and let rise in a warm place until doubled, about 45 minutes.

Preheat oven to 400° F.

Bake for about 30 minutes or until golden. Cool for 10 minutes on a wire rack. Whisk together powdered sugar, vanilla, and milk, adding more sugar or milk to obtain a consistency that drizzles off the whisk, and then drizzle with icing.

Old Milwaukee Rye Bread

David won the sweepstakes award in the bread club's first annual baking competition with this bread from America's Bread Book *by Mary Gubser. It takes several days to make, but the process is more about patience than effort.* **MAKES 2 ROUND LOAVES.**

Sponge

1	package active dry yeast
1½	cups warm water
2	cups rye flour
1	tablespoon caraway seeds

Dough

1	cup all-purpose flour
1	cup rye flour
1	package active dry yeast
1	tablespoon salt
1	tablespoon caraway seeds
1	cup water
¼	cup molasses
3	tablespoons shortening

> **DAVID'S BAKING TIPS**
>
> • Measure salt at the same time you measure yeast, and keep it in a small cup near the mixing bowl so you won't inadvertently forget to add it.
>
> • Check out bread cookbooks from a public library, and try a few recipes before deciding whether or not the books are worth the investment.
>
> • Learn to make one bread really well.

Two to three days before baking, mix yeast and warm water in a nonmetal mixing bowl, stirring until dissolved. With a wooden spoon mix in rye flour and caraway seeds. Cover loosely with plastic wrap and a towel, and set aside in a warm spot. The longer the sponge works, the more bite the bread will have. Stir twice a day; the aroma will be delicious.

On the third day, in a large bowl of a stand mixer, combine all-purpose flour, rye flour, yeast, salt, and caraway seeds, and blend well.

In a saucepan over medium heat, heat water, molasses, and shortening until warm. Shortening need not melt completely. Add to flour mixture, stirring well.

Stir down sponge, and add to flour mixture, beating well to blend. Using a dough hook, beat 3 minutes at medium speed. Gradually, add up to 2 cups of all-purpose flour to make a workable dough that pulls away from sides of bowl.

Turn out onto a lightly floured surface, and knead for about 10 minutes or until smooth and resilient. Place dough in a warm bowl brushed with melted shortening, turning to coat top. Cover loosely with plastic wrap and a towel, and let rise until doubled, about 1 hour.

Preheat oven to 375° F.

Brush a baking sheet with melted shortening, and sprinkle with cornmeal. Punch down dough, and divide in half. On a lightly floured surface shape each portion into a round loaf. Place loaves on baking sheet, cover with a cloth, and let rise 15 minutes. Slash each loaf ¼-inch deep with a razor blade. Cover and let rise 15 minutes more.

Bake for 40 to 45 minutes or until loaves sound hollow when tapped on bottom. Let cool on a wire rack.

Apple and Currant Bread Pudding

Here's a tempting way to use bread that's beginning to stale. **MAKES 9 TO 12 SERVINGS.**

6	large eggs, lightly beaten
1	cup lowfat milk
1½	tablespoons maple syrup
1	teaspoon vanilla extract
4	cups bread pieces or cubes (about 8 slices)

2 medium apples, peeled, cored, and sliced

1 cup currants

⅓ cup sugar

2 teaspoons cinnamon

½ teaspoon nutmeg

Preheat oven to 350° F.

In a medium mixing bowl beat eggs, and then add milk, maple syrup, and vanilla. Mix well. In a small bowl mix sugar, cinnamon, and nutmeg.

Spread half the bread pieces in a greased 9-by-9-inch pan. Add a layer of half the apple slices, half the currants, and half the sugar mixture. Repeat with remaining bread, apple, currants, and sugar mixture.

Give egg mixture a final stir, and pour over bread as evenly as possible, gently pressing to submerge bread. Bake for 40 to 50 minutes or until lightly browned and set. Let cool 10 minutes before serving in bowls. This is especially nice with a scoop of ice cream or drizzled with half-and-half. (You can also combine the ingredients the night before, store covered in the refrigerator, and then bake the next day.)

DAVID'S RECOMMENDED READING

• Eric Treuille and Ursula Ferrigno, *Ultimate Bread* (New York: DK Publishing, 1998). This book has good pictures and useful tips.

• Sunset publishing staff, *Breads*, 5th ed. (Menlo Park, CA: Sunset Books, 1994). This book, more widely known as the *Sunset Book of Breads*, is a classic that has gone through many editions with a wide variety of recipes in a no-nonsense format.

• Mary Gubser, *America's Bread Book: 300 Authentic Recipes for America's Homemade Breads, Collected on a 65,000-mile Journey through the Fifty United States* (New York: William Morrow and Company, 1985; New York: HarperTrade, 1992). Part cookbook and part travelogue, this book showcases breads from across the United States.

Carol Sturgeleski

TRUSTING OURSELVES

As for the earth, out of it cometh bread.

JOB 28:5

Carol Sturgeleski bakes because she wants to know. She wants to know where the flour comes from, how it was ground, where the salt was harvested, whether the sunflower seeds are organic.

"I'm a naturalist," she said, a word that's almost bigger than she is. It also means she's an avid reader of ingredient labels. "If I can't pronounce it, I don't eat it."

The philosophy has served her well. Forty years of baking bread have taken her more than halfway to seventy-one. She taught herself. "Being a homemaker with six kids, you didn't go out much," she said.

Carol has always liked working with her hands, but what's even more important for the home baker, she's learned to trust what they tell her. Hands, she's learned, are the filters between what we sense in our gut and what we read in a recipe. Putting that wisdom into practice is a matter of gaining experience, of knowing how a dough feels. For, like having to explain air, the words sometimes fail us.

For example, when I asked her the secret of her bread, she looked slightly perplexed, willing to help, but searching for words. She finally offered: "I read the recipe and whatever happens, happens." It's the sort of remark that can drive a novice to tears, especially anyone who's eaten the billowy clouds that she calls "cloverleaf rolls."

Maybe she knows too much. Maybe after decades of baking, she's too close to the challenges, so close that they no longer daunt her. But when you think about it, this is a good thing.

I think what Carol meant about surrendering to the recipe is that she believes a recipe will guide us to success if we trust our senses about how a dough looks and tastes and behaves. She goes slow, heeding the feel of the bread as she mixes in the flour and the liquids. "You can always add, but you can't take away," she explained. In other words, her best technique simply may be patience. "I believe if you can read, you can bake," she said. "Find the time. It's worth it."

Carol haunts the many excellent co-ops in St. Paul for her ingredients. In the corner of her sunlit kitchen sits a broad-shouldered Vitamix blender in which she grinds her own wheat berries for whole grain flour. She uses only sea salt in her breads and avoids any ingredient treated with preservatives.

She's an inveterate Earth Mother. "I always did things a little different," she said. "When I had babies, I nursed my babies," even as the rest of her neighbors were sterilizing bottles and mixing formula.

She still does things a little differently. She loves putting sautéed onions and garlic in her challah. Sometimes, she'll add some grated carrot for a golden color. She often puts her just-mixed bread dough into the refrigerator overnight, which slows down the yeast's fermentation to eke the most flavor from each cell. It's a tried-and-true technique, but her nonbaker friends think she's dreadfully inventive. "They think dough always has to be warm."

Carol found out about the St. Paul Bread Club when she was at the Mississippi Market Co-op on Selby Avenue and saw Klecko hosting a demonstration about sourdoughs. "I thought, 'Well, you never stop learning, no matter how old you are,'" she said, and has teamed up with him in demonstrations at the Minnesota State Fair, looking nothing so much as an elf next to the towering sprite that is Klecko.

Anyone can bake, she said, and we should, if only to gain a measure of control over how we care for our bodies. And there's no time like the present to begin. For in baking, she said, as in life, "What I've learned is that you have to learn by your mistakes. If at first you fail, try, try again. You will be blest!"

Challah

Klecko calls Carol the queen of challah. The classic recipe is lovely and took first place for challah at the 2004 bread club contest. But Carol likes to vary it by adding sautéed onion and garlic to the dough during the kneading process. This recipe is from the 1977 edition of Sunset's bread cookbook, now in its fifth edition. **MAKES 1 DOUBLE-BRAIDED LOAF.**

1	package active dry yeast
1¼	cups warm water
	Pinch saffron
1	teaspoon sea salt
¼	cup sugar
¼	cup vegetable or canola oil
2	large eggs, slightly beaten
5	to 5½ cups all-purpose flour, unsifted
1	medium onion, chopped (optional)
4	cloves garlic, minced (optional)
1	tablespoon canola oil (optional)
1	egg yolk beaten with 1 tablespoon water for egg wash
1	tablespoon sesame or poppy seeds, about

In a large bowl dissolve yeast in 1 cup water, and let sit until foamy, about 5 minutes. If adding onion and garlic, sauté onion in canola oil until translucent, add garlic, and then sauté 2 minutes longer. Set aside. In remaining ¼ cup water immerse saffron. Stir salt, sugar, oil, eggs, and saffron into yeast mixture. Gradually, beat in about 4½ cups flour to make a stiff dough.

Turn out onto a lightly floured surface, and knead until smooth and shiny. This may take anywhere from 5 to 20 minutes. (Knead in onion and garlic if using.) Add flour as needed to prevent sticking. Turn dough into an oiled bowl, turning to coat top. Cover with plastic wrap, and let rise in a warm place until doubled, about 1½ hours. Punch dough down, and knead briefly on a lightly floured board to release air. Set aside about ¾ cup dough and cover.

Divide remaining dough into 4 equal portions, and roll each to form a rope about 20 inches long. Place strips lengthwise on a greased baking sheet, pinch tops together, and braid as follows: pick up the strand on the right, and bring it over the next one, under the third, and over the fourth. Repeat motion, always starting with strand on right, until braid is complete. Pinch ends together, and tuck under.

Roll reserved dough into a rope about 15 inches long, cut into 3 ropes, and make a small, 3-strand braid. Lay along top center of large braid. Cover with a cloth, and let rise in a warm place until almost doubled, about 1 hour.

Preheat oven to 350° F.

Using a soft brush or your fingers, spread egg wash evenly over braid, and sprinkle with seeds. Bake for 30 to 35 minutes or until loaf is golden brown and sounds hollow when tapped on bottom. Cool on a wire rack.

Hearty Honey Wheat Bread

It's amazing how many variations there are on the theme of wheat bread. Sweeteners vary. Some add fats; others don't. Some are a purist's loaf, whereas others mix and match different flours. This is one of the combination wheat breads, with a duet of sweeteners and a trio of flours. **MAKES 2 LOAVES.**

1	package active dry yeast
2½	cups warm water
1	teaspoon sea salt
½	cup honey
⅓	cup light molasses
⅓	cup olive oil or softened unsalted butter
2½ to 4	cups unbleached all-purpose flour
2½	cup whole wheat flour
1½	cup medium rye flour

In a large bowl of a mixer, dissolve yeast in warm water, and wait until it foams, about 5 minutes. Measure 1½ cups all-purpose flour and all the whole wheat flour by lightly spooning into a measuring cup and leveling off, and then add to yeast mixture along with salt, honey, molasses, and olive oil or butter.

Mix at low speed until moistened and then at medium speed for 3 minutes. Stir in rye flour, and gradually add enough all-purpose flour until dough pulls cleanly away from sides of bowl.

Turn out onto a lightly floured surface, and knead until smooth and elastic, adding flour as necessary, about 10 minutes. Place dough in a greased bowl, turning to coat top, cover with plastic wrap, and let rise in a warm place until doubled, about 1½ hours.

Punch down dough several times to deflate air bubbles, divide in half, and then shape into loaves. Place shaped loaves into two greased loaf pans, cover with a cloth, and let rise in a warm place until doubled, about 45 minutes.

Preheat oven to 350° F.

Bake for 35 to 45 minutes or until loaves sound hollow when lightly tapped on bottom. Remove from pans immediately, and cool on wire rack.

CAROL'S BAKING TIPS

• During a Minnesota winter, it's sometimes difficult to find a warm enough place in which to let your dough rise. So turn on your oven to 200° F for about a minute, turn it off, and then set your bread in the now slightly warmed chamber to rise. Just make sure you remember to turn off the oven!

• When it comes to salt, it doesn't make a lot of difference whether you use table, kosher, or sea salt. But it does make a little difference, enough so that I favor sea salt, which is evaporated from sea water instead of mined from dry beds. It costs a little more, but it's "saltier."

Glazed Bubble Ring

This is a great recipe for introducing kids to the joys of making bread. Once the dough has risen, let them help you shape the balls and dip them in butter and the topping mixture. Once baked, it's as much fun to pull the balls apart and eat them. **MAKES 1 TEN-INCH RING.**

Dough

    2   packages active dry yeast
    ½   cup warm water
    2   cups lowfat milk, scalded
    ½   cup sugar
    6   tablespoons shortening
    2   teaspoons salt
    6   to 7 cups all-purpose flour
    2   large eggs, well beaten

Topping

    ½   cup sugar
    ½   cup finely chopped nuts (optional)
    ½   cup raisins
    1   teaspoon cinnamon
    ⅓   cup unsalted butter

Glaze

    1   cup powdered sugar, sifted
    ½   teaspoon vanilla
    1   tablespoon lowfat milk

In a small bowl dissolve yeast and water, and let foam, about 5 minutes. Scald milk by heating in a saucepan until bubbles begin to appear around edge. In a large bowl pour hot milk over sugar, shortening, and salt, and cool to lukewarm. Blend in 1 cup flour, and beat until smooth. Stir in yeast mixture. Add half remaining flour, and beat until very smooth. Beat in eggs and then enough flour to make a soft dough.

Turn out onto a lightly floured surface, and knead until smooth and elastic. Place in an oiled bowl, turning to coat top. Cover with plastic wrap, and let rise in a warm place until doubled, about 1 hour.

Punch down dough, and turn out onto a lightly floured surface. Divide dough into 20 equal portions, and shape into balls.

Combine sugar, nuts, raisins, and cinnamon. Melt butter in a small dish. Dip each ball into butter, roll in sugar mixture, and then arrange in a well-greased 10-inch tube pan. Cover with a cloth, and let rise until doubled, about 30 minutes.

Preheat oven to 350° F.

Bake for 35 minutes or until well browned. Cool in pan 10 minutes, remove from pan, and then turn right side up on wire rack. To make glaze, whisk together milk, vanilla, and powdered sugar; drizzle over bubbles.

Cloverleaf Rolls

Carol said that if you want fresh rolls at noon, make and form the rolls the night before, covering the muffin tins with plastic wrap and immediately placing them in the refrigerator. The next morning take them out, replace the plastic wrap with a cloth, and let them rise until doubled. Bake as directed. **MAKES 24 ROLLS.**

1	package active dry yeast
¼	cup warm water
¾	cup lowfat milk, scalded
½	cup shortening
½	cup sugar
1	teaspoon salt
3	large eggs, beaten
4½	cups all-purpose flour, sifted

In a small bowl dissolve yeast in warm water, and let foam, about 5 minutes. Scald milk by heating in a saucepan until bubbles begin to appear around edge. Pour hot milk over shortening, sugar, and salt, and let cool to lukewarm. Add yeast mixture, and mix well. Add eggs and flour, mixing to make a smooth, soft dough.

Turn out onto a lightly floured surface, and knead gently, about 5 minutes. Place in an oiled bowl, turning once to coat top. Cover with plastic wrap, and let rise until doubled.

Punch down dough, and turn out onto a lightly floured surface. Grease 2 muffin tins. Shape dough into 1-inch balls, and arrange 3 in each cup. Cover with a cloth, and let rise until very light and puffy.

Preheat oven to 400° F.

Bake for 15 minutes. Turn out onto a wire rack.

CAROL'S RECOMMENDED READING

• *Sunset Book of Breads* (Menlo Park, CA: Sunset Books, 1966). This book is now available in a new edition: Sunset publishing staff, *Breads*, 5th ed. (1994).

• Red Star Yeast, *Red Star Centennial Bread Sampler*

• Pillsbury editors, *Pillsbury Best of the Bake-off Cookbook: Recipes from America's Favorite Cooking Contest* (Hoboken, NJ: John Wiley and Sons, 2004).

Mark Shafer

BAKING IMPROVISATION

Bread plays an important part in the preparation of attractive and appetizing meals. Nearly every meal offers the use for toast in some delicious form, and because toasting so adds flavor and nourishment to good bread, its use is to be encouraged.

THE W. E. LONG COMPANY, MAKERS OF HOLSUM BREAD, FROM A TURN-OF-THE-CENTURY PAMPHLET

Mark Shafer is of the "Oh, wait, maybe . . . " school of bread making. As in, "Oh, wait, maybe I'll throw in some molasses." Or, "Oh, wait, maybe I'll throw in some leftover potatoes." Or here's a favorite: "Oh, wait, maybe I'll throw in the crumbs left in that box of Shredded Wheat."

How does he know how much to measure?

"Measure?"

From the other side of the room, his wife Judy burst out laughing. "He doesn't do that."

"I'm basically a 'from scratch' person," Mark said, almost apologetically, perhaps sensing that a novice baker could view his culinary improv either as a lifeline or as a deal breaker. He'd be right on both counts. If you think his philosophy means that bread is as much art as it is craft, then it's a lifeline.

But the deal breaker aspect lurks. A beginner craves logic, boundaries, consistency—in other words, a recipe. They say you can never step in the same river twice, and we hear that as a metaphor for possibility. So why does the notion of never making the same loaf twice make us feel intimidated and resigned to spending our children's inheritance at the neighborhood artisans' bakery?

The solution is experience. After a few loaves you grow less wary and more curious about how that batch will respond. Dough, at heart, is far more welcoming than it is temperamental. Mark, sixty-three, can "oh, wait" his way through a recipe because he has thirty years' experience beneath his palms. Even after his son bought him a burly Kitchen Aid mixer, he still tends to mix his dough by hand. As with so many bread bakers, the tangible connection provides an elemental satisfaction. But it also serves a purpose.

"You never know what your flour is going to be like that day," he said, adding that he favors the Hodgson Mill brand. And so he adds and adjusts, kneads and knows.

His impulse to begin making bread came rather suddenly. In 1974 bread expert Bernard Clayton was at the J. C. Penney store in Rosedale promoting his *Complete Book of Breads*. Mark and Judy decided on a whim to go see him. Mark listened, considered, and bought, and "then I went home that day and baked my first loaf of bread."

Nice story, but there was more than mere whim at work. After all, he'd saved the large aluminum bread proofing box that his mother had always used. "It was very rare to have commercial bread in our house," he said of growing up in West St. Paul not far from where he now lives. "I can remember the lid being pushed up by the dough and her having to scrape it down."

Mark's favorite breads are whole wheat varieties, sturdy loaves sweetened with honey and developed by hard labor and the ability to confront the dough's stickiness head-on instead of showering it with flour. "You have to whack the bread," Mark said, "That's what Clayton says. Don't be gentle with the dough."

He described a process of throwing the dough down on the counter, gathering it up, and then flinging it down again and again until it starts, imperceptibly at first, to firm up and grow smooth.

It is not unknown for the household to be awakened by the sound of a blob of dough being thwacked against a counter. There are worse ways to wake up.

Cheddar Cheese Bread

This bread makes terrific toast, and a great base for chicken a la king or sautéed and creamed mushrooms. It's from the 1973 edition of The Complete Book of Breads *by Bernard Clayton.* **MAKES 2 LOAVES.**

1	package active dry yeast
¼	cup warm water
1¾	cups lowfat milk
¼	cup sugar
2	teaspoons salt
2	tablespoons unsalted butter
3	cups sharp Cheddar cheese, shredded
5½	cups all-purpose or bread flour

In a small bowl dissolve yeast in warm water, and set aside until foamy, about 5 minutes. Scald milk by heating in a saucepan until bubbles begin to appear around edge. Remove from heat, and stir in sugar, salt, butter, and 2 cups Cheddar. Stir until melted. Set aside, and cool to lukewarm.

In a mixing bowl combine 2½ cups flour, cheese mixture, yeast, and remaining cheese. With an electric mixer at medium speed for 2 minutes or with a wooden spoon for 150 strong strokes, beat batter until smooth.

Add additional flour, 1 cup at a time, stirring with a wooden spoon and then by hand, until dough is rough formed and no longer sticks to sides of bowl. Turn out onto a lightly floured surface, and knead with a strong push-turn-fold motion until smooth and elastic. Place in an oiled bowl, turning to coat top, cover with plastic wrap, and let rise until doubled.

Punch down dough, turn out onto a floured surface, and divide in half. Shape each half into a ball, cover with a cloth, and let rest for 10 minutes. Flatten each with your fist, fold in half, and pinch seams tightly together. Place in greased baking pans, seam side down. Cover with a cloth, and let rise in a warm place until doubled, about 1 hour. It will rise about 1 inch above the edge of the pans.

Preheat oven to 375° F.

Bake for 40 minutes. This bread browns easily because of the butterfat in the cheese, so watch it closely after the first 15 minutes. If necessary, cover loaves with foil to keep from getting too brown. Turn out of pans, and let cool on a wire rack.

Sugarplum Bread

This holiday bread can double as a centerpiece on a brunch table, with its small sugarplums surrounding the main loaf. That is, until it disappears, which doesn't take long. This is from The Complete Book of Breads *by Bernard Clayton.* **MAKES 1 LARGE AND 6 BABY LOAVES.**

> 5 to 5½ cups all-purpose flour
> ½ cup sugar
> 1½ teaspoons salt
> 2 packages active dry yeast
> ⅓ cup nonfat dry milk
> 1⅓ cups warm water
> ¼ cup shortening
> 2 large eggs, beaten
> ½ teaspoon vanilla
> ¼ teaspoon nutmeg
> ½ cup candied mixed fruits and peels
> 1 cup seedless raisins
> 1 cup powdered sugar
> 1 tablespoon fresh-squeezed lemon juice
> Candied cherries and walnut halves for garnish

In a large bowl combine 2 cups flour with sugar, salt, yeast, milk, and water. Blend thoroughly, and add shortening, eggs, vanilla, nutmeg, mixed fruits and peels, and raisins. Stir with a wooden spoon or an electric mixer at medium speed for 2 minutes.

Stir in remaining flour, ½ cup at a time, first with a spoon and then by hand. The dough will be a rough, shaggy mass that will clean the sides of the bowl. If dough continues to be moist and sticky, add several sprinkles of flour.

Turn out onto a lightly floured surface, and knead until smooth and elastic; bubbles will rise under surface. Sprinkle with additional flour if sticky. Occasionally, throw hard against the counter, and then resume kneading, about 8 minutes total.

Place in an oiled bowl, turning to coat top, cover with plastic wrap, and let rise in a warm place until doubled, 1 to 2 hours.

Divide in half, and knead each piece for about 30 seconds. Shape first piece into a ball, flatten slightly on top, and place on a greased baking sheet. Divide second portion into 6 pieces, and shape each into a ball. Place in greased muffin cups, and press down until almost level with top of cups.

Cover with a cloth, and let rise in a warm place until doubled, about 30 minutes.

Preheat oven to 350° F.

Bake large loaf for 35 minutes and smaller loaves for 20 minutes, until bread sounds hollow when tapped on bottom. Turn small loaves out of muffin cups, and place on a wire rack to cool. To make confectioners' icing, whisk together powdered sugar and lemon juice. Frost large loaf with a drizzle of icing, and garnish with candied cherries. For small loaves drizzle tops, and cap each with a perfect walnut half.

Sunset White Bread

It's an indication of how much our bread tastes have changed that this recipe is one of only a very few for white bread shared by these bakers. But this is the classic, Mark's favorite and a staple of Sunset *magazine's recipe collection. It's open to endless variations of ingredients—this is the bread for your imagination—but the purist's version is where a beginning baker should start. This bread makes great toast and freezes well double-wrapped in plastic.* **MAKES 2 LOAVES.**

  1 package active dry yeast
 ¼ cup warm water
  2 cups lowfat milk, warmed
  3 tablespoons unsalted butter, melted
  1 tablespoon salt
  2 tablespoons sugar
  5 to 6 cups all-purpose flour

In a large mixing bowl dissolve yeast in water, and let stand until foamy, about 5 minutes. Stir in warm milk, melted butter, salt, and sugar, and blend well. Stir in 3 cups flour, 1 cup at a time. Beat 50 strokes. Add 1 cup flour, and beat until smooth. Work in 1 cup flour more with fingers. Dough should be a rough mass, pulling clear of sides of bowl.

Turn out onto a well-floured surface, and knead, adding only as much remaining flour as necessary. Keeping hands floured, knead dough until soft and satiny and no longer sticky, about 10 minutes. Place in an oiled bowl, turning to coat top, cover with plastic wrap, and let rise in a warm place until doubled, about 1½ hours. Test by poking with finger. If dent remains, dough is risen.

Punch down, and knead out air bubbles. Divide in half, and press each piece into a rough oval as long as your loaf pan. Fold together in thirds, like a business

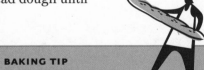

MARK'S BAKING TIP

• You can get the best leverage for kneading if your surface is only as high as your downstretched arms. There's less back strain, and you can really get that push-turn-fold rhythm going. Mark built a special countertop in his kitchen just for kneading.

letter, pinch seam closed, and place in a greased loaf pan, seam side down. Cover with a cloth, and let rise until doubled, about 45 minutes.

Preheat oven to 375° F.

Bake for 45 minutes or until loaves sound hollow when thumped on bottom. Turn out bread from pans, and let cool on a wire rack.

Buttermilk Whole Wheat Bread

In this streamlined recipe the dough need rise only once, and that's in the pans. Mark likes to use two rises: once in a covered bowl until doubled and again in pans. The use of baking soda in addition to yeast and the warm buttermilk give this loaf a gentle tang. Mark adapted this recipe from Bernard Clayton's The Complete Book of Breads. **MAKES 2 LOAVES.**

2	packages active dry yeast
¾	cup warm water
1¼	cups buttermilk, room temperature
1½	cups all-purpose flour
3	cups whole wheat flour
¼	cup canola oil or unsalted butter
2	tablespoons brown sugar or molasses
2	teaspoons baking powder
2	teaspoons salt
1	tablespoon unsalted butter, melted

In the large bowl of a mixer, dissolve yeast in water, and let stand until foamy, about 5 minutes. Add buttermilk, all-purpose flour, 1 cup whole wheat flour, oil or butter, brown sugar or molasses, baking powder, and salt. Blend on low speed until dry ingredients are absorbed.

Scrape down bowl, and increase speed to medium for 2 minutes. Stop mixer. With a wooden spoon stir in remaining whole wheat flour, ½ cup at a time. When it becomes too thick, work in flour by hand. Let dough rest, about 4 minutes, allowing flour to fully absorb liquid. Dough will be slightly sticky and soft. Add an additional ¼ cup whole wheat flour if too sticky.

Turn out onto a well-floured surface, and using a bench knife or a wide spatula to scrape counter clean as you lift and fold, knead until beginning to firm up. Occasionally lift dough and bang down hard. Knead for about 8 minutes.

Divide in half, cover with a cloth, and let rest for 5 minutes. Roll or press into a rectangle as long as your loaf pan. Roll up like a jellyroll, and pinch shut seam and ends. Place in a greased loaf pan, and brush lightly with melted butter. Cover with wax paper, and let rise in a warm place until 1 to 2 inches above edge of pan, about 1 hour.

Preheat oven to 425° F.

Bake for 30 to 35 minutes or until loaves sound hollow when thumped on bottom. Cover with foil if crusts brown too rapidly. Turn out of pans, and let cool on a wire rack.

Foster and Elaine Cole

FROM THE LAND

Whose bread I eat, his song I sing.

GERMAN PROVERB

Here, in the upper Midwest, we live among bread's raw ingredients. Bordering fields of wheat, oats, barley, flax, corn, and soybeans are milled into flour. Beekeepers tend their stark white filing cabinets of honey, the bees themselves plying our orchards and gardens. The air teems with invisible spores of yeast.

Granted, we have to look elsewhere for salt. But when it comes to water, well, to keep counting past 10,000 just feels like we're rubbing it in.

This is the landscape that Foster and Elaine Cole explore in their quest for local ingredients. "I really, really like to eat honey on bread," said Foster, which led them to discover Don Johnston's honey business in Rochester, where the different varieties are treated as carefully as varietals of wine.

Their desire for homegrown goods also led them to Great River Organic Milling in Fountain City, Wisconsin, an effort in sustainable agriculture where a farm's grains are raised, milled, and sold in strikingly elegant packages that feature a blue heron. The ingredients for wonderful bread are right here, as much a part of the community as we are.

The Coles work as a team. "Elaine finds a lot of things, I follow up on how I can use it, and off we go," Foster said. "One of the things we like about baking bread is how it's broadened our interests and where it leads us." They urge anyone with a passion for bread to visit the museum at the American Institute of Baking in Manhattan, Kansas. And they always consult Maggie Glezer's list of great bakeries in her classic book *Artisan Baking* when they visit another city.

But it's their gentle obsession with honey that's led them in the most interesting directions. Foster, a child psychologist, has taken a weekend beekeeping course at the University of Minnesota—not that their neighbors in New Brighton ever will see hives in their backyard. "I wanted to know how the different pollen sources affect the flavor," he said, describing how honeys differ depending on what is in bloom at the time, whether basswood trees or blackberry bushes.

Then there's buckwheat honey—"which is like getting whacked with a two-by-four," Elaine said.

In 2005 Foster's love of the stuff led him to enter a loaf of honey-laced bread in the baking contest of the Minnesota State Fair's bee and honey division. He took second place, besting well-known veterans of State Fair baking contests. He was stunned; Elaine was smitten. "I went around pretending to say to everyone, 'Hello, have you met my husband? He took second place in the bread competition.'"

Foster, forty-four, began baking bread years ago after Elaine gave him *Bread Alone* by Daniel Leader and Judith Blahnik. "I made the basic recipe maybe twenty times until I felt I'd learned all about it," he said, a practice he encourages all beginning bakers to follow.

Elaine, forty-five, a financial analyst, concentrates more on tracking down interesting ingredients. Yet she tackled the elaborate method for making a liquid sourdough that Nancy Silverton describes in *Breads from the La Brea Bakery*. ("On the fourth day, the mixture may begin to turn a brownish-purple, and it may seethe with large bubbles.")

They don't bake together but rather complement each other: She'll make the main dish; he'll bake an accompanying bread. It's an unconscious division of labor that, nonetheless, is mirrored in the makeup of the St. Paul Bread Club. It's dangerous to read too much into gender, but Foster was surprised, as many are, by the number of men in the club.

Granted, the baking profession has long been dominated by men. "Guys usually are more into the technical angle of things, and if you want that, it's there," Foster said. "Bread has a greater margin for error than in, say, making pastries." But as far as he's concerned, he just likes bread.

For years they've used their Kitchen Aid mixer to grind their own wheat berries using a special attachment—a hefty beauty that even has a millpond scene on the control knob. That's about as elaborate as their equipment gets. Except for one gadget that is as big as, well, their house.

"Here in Minnesota, you really can use your house as a tool," he said.

It's not so much a choice as a necessity, given the vagaries of our seasons. In the summer he'll set his dough down in the cool basement to slow down its rising, which improves the flavor. In the winter, though, the dough gets a boost by proofing in one of the kitchen cupboards built against a heating vent. "And we treat the garage like a walk-in cooler."

It's the philosophy of acting locally, taken to its most domestic conclusion.

FOSTER AND ELAINE'S BAKING TIPS

• Clear plastic hair-processing caps make great reusable covers for bowls, pans, and baskets while dough is rising. Do not use shower caps made from heavy, opaque vinyl, however, as the odor may taint the dough and the color obscure your view of the rising dough.

• If your loaves look skimpy after rising in 9-by-5-by-3-inch bread pans, use an 8½-by-4½-by-2¾-inch loaf pan the next time. The smaller pan will fill better when the dough rises, making for a higher, more handsome loaf. The difference in dimensions seems small, but the effect can be large.

• Buy a baking stone for your oven. Baking on a stone leads to more crusty bread and more crisp pizza crust. Preheat the stone for forty-five minutes to an hour before baking bread on it. Even bread baked in loaf pans will develop a nicer bottom if placed directly on the stone.

• When making free-form bread, let it rise on parchment paper placed on a baking sheet. The parchment makes it easy to slide the dough onto a baking stone without the dough sticking to the sheet or the wooden peel. You can pull the parchment out from under the bread after the bread has firmed up or simply leave it between the bread and the stone for the entire baking period.

• For a distinctive look let the dough rise in willow dough-rising baskets (*brotform*) instead of in loaf pans. Before placing the dough into the basket, spray the basket with a nonstick cooking spray and lightly dust it with flour. When the dough has risen, turn it out of the *brotform* and onto a baking stone.

Honey Whole Grain Bread

Here's Foster's State Fair winner, which he adapted from a recipe for whole wheat millet bread that first appeared in The Chicago Tribune Cookbook *in 1989.* **MAKES 2 LOAVES.**

- ½ cup honey
- 2 packages active dry yeast
- 1¾ cups warm water
- 3 cups coarse-ground whole wheat flour
- ¼ cup bulgur
- ¼ cup canola oil
- 1 tablespoon kosher salt
- ¾ cup millet
- 2 to 2½ cups bread flour

Make a sponge by dissolving honey and yeast in warm water in a large bowl; let stand until bubbly, about 5 minutes. Add whole wheat flour, bulgur, oil, and salt, and mix until smooth. Cover with plastic wrap, and let rise about 1 hour or in the refrigerator overnight. If overnight rise is used, let sponge warm up for at least 2 hours before proceeding.

Stir in millet and bread flour until a firm dough forms. Turn out onto a lightly floured surface, and knead until smooth and elastic. Place in an oiled bowl, turning to coat top, cover with plastic wrap, and let rise until doubled, about 1 hour.

Deflate dough, cover, and let rise again until doubled, about 1 hour. Deflate dough, cut in half, and shape the pieces into 2 loaves. Place in oiled loaf pans. Cover with a cloth, and let rise 1 hour.

Preheat oven to 350° F.

Bake for 40 to 45 minutes or until nicely browned. Turn out onto wire racks to cool.

Whole Grain Hamburger Buns

These buns will hold up to any filling you favor, from the juiciest grilled hamburgers to a thick slice of the perfect summer tomato topped with a dollop of mayonnaise. The Coles developed this recipe in their kitchen.

MAKES 12 BUNS.

2	cups bread flour
¾	cup whole wheat flour
1	cup mixture of whole grains and seeds (mix to taste with, e.g., oat groats, rolled oats, millet, bulgur, hot cereal mix, polenta, and poppy or sunflower seeds)
2	tablespoons sugar
2	teaspoons salt
½	cup dry potato flakes
¼	cup nonfat dry milk
1	tablespoon vital wheat gluten
2¼	teaspoons instant yeast
1½	cups warm water
¼	cup canola oil
1	tablespoon malt syrup

In a large bowl mix dry ingredients, reserving ¼ cup bread flour. Add water, and stir for 1 minute. Add oil and malt syrup, and stir vigorously for 2 minutes. Let sit covered for 15 minutes.

Turn out onto a lightly floured surface, and knead for several minutes, adding just enough remaining bread flour, 1 tablespoon at a time, until dough is elastic but still slightly sticky. Shape dough into a ball, and place in an oiled bowl, turning to coat. Cover with plastic wrap, and let rise until doubled, about 1 hour.

Gently deflate dough by turning out onto counter. Cut into 12 equal pieces, and shape each piece into a ball. To shape, fold each piece in half, tucking under the ends and pinching them together. Working on an unfloured surface, cup your hand over the dough and move the ball in small circles. The friction will cause the seam to close and the surface to stretch into a smooth sphere. Cover and let rest for 10 minutes.

Flatten each ball into a circle about 3½ inches across and ½ inch thick. Place each piece of dough on a baking sheet that's been oiled or covered with parchment paper. Press thumb into the middle of each bun, leaving a slight indentation. Cover with a warm, damp cloth, and let rise over a pan of hot water in an oven for 1 hour.

Remove buns from the oven, and preheat to 400° F.

Bake for 20 minutes. Cool on a wire rack.

Buttermilk Bulgur Bread

This recipe originally appeared in The Grains Cookbook *by the late Bert Greene. Greene describes this bread as "the kind your grandmother served when you stayed over" and begs those enjoying the bread to "try it toasted, please!"* **MAKES 2 MEDIUM LOAVES,** *although Foster sometimes makes 4 mini loaves; if you prefer them, bake only 15 minutes. If you prefer using powdered buttermilk, convert the water and the buttermilk to an equivalent 1¾ cups water, and mix in ¼ cup plus 2 tablespoons powdered buttermilk.*

1	package active dry yeast
¼	cup warm water
3	tablespoons honey
2	teaspoons tomato paste
½	cup fine-ground bulgur
1½	cups buttermilk, warmed
⅓	cup unsalted butter, melted
1	teaspoon kosher salt
2	cups whole wheat flour
2	cups bread flour, about

In a large bowl dissolve yeast in water, and let stand until yeast softens, about 5 minutes. Add honey and tomato paste, and whisk until smooth. Stir in bulgur and buttermilk; let stand 20 minutes.

Add butter and salt. Stir in whole wheat flour and about 1½ cups bread flour to make a stiff dough. Turn out onto a lightly floured surface, and knead for 15 minutes, adding more flour if necessary. Place in a lightly oiled bowl, turning to coat top, cover with plastic wrap, and let rise until doubled, about 1½ hours.

Turn out onto a lightly floured surface, punch down, and divide into desired number of large or small loaves. Shape and place on a baking sheet sprinkled with cornmeal or in greased mini loaf pans. Brush loaves lightly with water, cover with a cloth, and let rise in a warm place until doubled, about 45 minutes.

Preheat oven to 400° F.

With a sharp knife slash surface of loaves, and then brush again with water. Bake large loaves for about 25 minutes, mini loaves for 15 minutes, or until crisp and hollow sounding when tapped with finger. Cool on a wire rack.

Pane di Como

Pane di como (pahna dee CO-mo) is one of Foster's favorites. He loves its "fresh floury smell," and it has a great crust. It's from The Italian Baker *by Carol Field. Malt syrup, also called barley malt syrup, is available in co-ops and some grocery stores. This bread is best started the night before you intend to bake.* **MAKES 2 ROUND LOAVES.**

Starter

- 1 teaspoon active dry yeast
- 1 scant teaspoon malt syrup
- ⅓ cup warm water
- ⅔ cup lowfat milk, room temperature
- 1 cup unbleached all-purpose flour

Dough

    2   cups water, room temperature
    6¼   cups unbleached all-purpose flour
    1   tablespoon salt

Stir yeast and malt into water, and let stand until foamy, about 10 minutes. Stir in milk, and beat in flour with a wooden spoon for about 100 strokes until smooth. Cover with plastic wrap, and let stand on your kitchen counter until bubbly, at least 4 hours but preferably overnight.

Add water to starter; mix and squeeze between fingers until fairly well broken up. In a separate bowl mix flour and salt, and then stir 2 cups at a time into starter mixture. When too stiff to mix with a wooden spoon, just plunge in with your hands. Mix until well blended, about 4 to 5 minutes. Knead on a well-floured surface until elastic but still moist and tacky. Once it has come together nicely, crash it down vigorously on the work surface to develop the gluten.

Place in an oiled bowl, turning to coat top. Cover with plastic wrap, and let rise until doubled, about 1½ hours. Turn out onto a floured surface, cut in half, and then shape into 2 round loaves. Place smooth side down in baskets lined with generously floured kitchen towels. Cover with towels, and let rise until fully doubled.

Preheat oven to 400° F, with baking stone, 30 minutes before baking. Sprinkle stone with cornmeal, if desired.

Very carefully invert loaves onto stone, and bake until a loaf sounds hollow when the bottom is tapped, about 50 minutes. Cool on wire racks.

Lauren "Lorenzo" Allen

DO NOT FEAR BIG FLAVORS

When I finish my approximately two hundred loaves each day, I do not credit magic! I credit my strength, my endurance, knowledge, science, and my endless curiosity for the physics and chemistry of bread.

LAURA HOLLAND, BAKER

Lauren "Lorenzo" Allen is Klecko's right-hand man for the bread club. A baker at the St. Agnes Baking Company, Lorenzo works on the specialty breads and more elaborate orders. Baking was not a place he had imagined ending up, but at the age of twenty-eight, he said he'll be doing it forever.

The Allen family has been a part of Twin Cities' restaurants for most of Lorenzo's life. His parents were in on the early pre-franchise days of Green Mill Pizza and eventually went on to open Maggiore in Woodbury. It featured authentic Italian cuisine, black tablecloths, and a pioneering concept in wine dinners, being one of the first restaurants here to pair a different wine with each course. It may have been a little ahead of its time, closing in 1999. They now do restaurant consulting and hotel management.

Lorenzo wanted to be a chef or a consultant and moved to Italy to immerse himself in its culture. He went to the Italian Culinary Institute for Foreigners, where he fell in love with pastries and desserts. He also learned more than he realized at the time.

"I came back still wanting to be a chef, but what I'd learned wasn't really applicable here," he said. Diners might say they want authentic Italian cuisine while turning out to be far more comfortable when the authenticity comes in the dessert course rather than in the entrée.

He got a job at Pazzaluna, in downtown St. Paul, where his duties included making a daily selection of breads. "I enjoyed doing that day in and day out," he said. "It kind of snuck up on me." He considered his Italian education with a fresh eye. "Sometimes, you don't realize everything you've learned for quite a while."

He realized that his future was in bread and set about seeking a mentor. He'd heard of a guy named Klecko who was taking bread seriously. "He looked a little off his rocker, which I liked, so I started pestering him." Eventually, the match was made.

Lorenzo is all about big flavors. He makes a black pepper loaf that he warns people about before they take their first bite. His recommendation for the amount of poppy seeds to put in his loaf of Buttermilk Poppyseed Bread could make you flunk a workplace drug test if you were fortunate enough to have some for breakfast.

While among the youngest people in the room during meetings of the bread club, he quietly offers up words of encouragement like an elder: "Don't consider a dough a failure if it didn't work out 'perfectly' the first two times you make it," he said. "Consider that learning. Now you're more familiar with it. Now what happens?"

"Commercial bakeries," he also said, "put hours and hours into testing out new doughs. They have people with years of experience, degrees, and big salaries working this out. If you can get a dough from page to pan in two tries, that's fantastic! If not, don't be discouraged."

Above all, he added—and you can almost see the bumper sticker— "Do not fear the yeast!"

LORENZO'S BAKING TIPS

· Don't be a slave to diversity. Find a favorite dough, and work with it until you own it. Know how it behaves throughout the year. Be able to mix it without peeking at the formula. After all that, *then* play around with the ingredients.

· Always preheat your oven well ahead of time. A bread meant to be baked at 375° F but started at 286° F will never work out right.

· Ask yourself, Am I enjoying baking? Keep it fun!

Lorenzo's Grissini

These are not your run-of-the-mill (odd phrase, that), spongy takeout-pizza-style breadsticks but crispy, pencil-thin sticks that can double as a table's centerpiece. But the real joy of these grissini is in the flavors. While adding the olive oil, toss in fresh thyme, crushed red peppers, freshly grated pecorino cheese, or a smear of roasted garlic.

Grissini should be baked slowly, at between 250° F and 280° F. It'll take at least an hour to get them perfectly crisp; two hours is not out of the question. If they are underbaked, they'll stale in about six hours.

But baked properly and stored airtight, they'll keep for weeks with no major flavor loss. In fact, like the classic biscotti cookie, they're perfect for making in large amounts every once in a while because they're designed to keep for the duration of, say, a journey to the other side of the mountains—or a trip up the North Shore. **MAKES LOTS.**

1	tablespoon active dry yeast
2¾	cups warm water
1	tablespoon honey
4½	cups semolina flour
3	cups bread flour
1½	tablespoons salt
1	tablespoon extra-virgin olive oil
	Additional flavorings (see note above)

In a large bowl dissolve yeast and honey in water, and let stand until foamy, about 5 minutes. Add flours gradually, mixing well. Then add salt, and continue mixing until dough forms a ball. Drizzle in olive oil and add any additional flavorings. Cover with plastic wrap, and let sit for at least 2 and even 4 hours. The flavor and texture improve if dough is allowed to rise until it falls.

Preheat oven to 275° F.

Take a pinch of dough, and roll pencil thin as long as your baking sheet. You will soon learn how much dough you need. Rolling the *grissini* is easier if your surface is barely, if at all, floured. Keep dough covered. Bake for 1 to 2 hours.

Buttermilk Poppy Seed Bread

This is a striking bread that should be placed whole on the table and sliced with the meal. Its gentle curve and trademark eleven slashes are reminiscent of a concertina in mid-serenade. **MAKES 1 LARGE OR 2 SMALL LOAVES.**

4½ to 5 cups bread flour
2 packages active dry yeast
2¾ cups buttermilk, room temperature
2 teaspoons honey
2 teaspoons sea salt
2 teaspoons olive oil
½ to 1 cup poppy seeds

In a large bowl whisk together 4½ cups flour and yeast, and make a well in center. In a small bowl whisk together buttermilk, honey, and olive oil. Pour into well, and begin stirring, bringing in flour from sides to form a ball of dough. Add salt and desired amount of poppy seeds, and mix well.

Turn out onto a lightly floured surface, and knead until smooth and springy, about 10 minutes, adding additional ½ cup flour if necessary. Place in an oiled bowl, turning to coat top, cover with plastic wrap, and let rise until doubled, about 1 hour.

Turn out onto a lightly floured surface, and shape loaves into desired size. Do not taper at ends. Place on a baking sheet covered with parchment paper, and then bend down ends to give loaves a slight curve. Dust with flour, and then slash 11 times across top at a slight angle. Cover with a cloth, and let rise until doubled, about 1 hour.

Preheat oven to 375° F.

Bake for 30 to 40 minutes or until golden brown. Cool on a wire rack.

Babas au Rhum

Babas au rhum *(BAH-ba-o-rum) was brought to Paris by the deposed king of Poland in the 1600s. According to legend, he found the Polish* kugelhopf *too dry and began dipping his bread in rum, which so delighted him that he named the cake after one of the heroes of his favorite book,* Ali Baba, *from* A Thousand and One Nights. *Later, his baker refined the sweet bread by using brioche dough and adding currants. In France* baba *came to mean "falling over or dizzy."*

Babas in their rum syrup can remain good for close to a year. But they won't last that long. They're best served with fresh whipped cream and fresh sliced fruit or berries. Most of what's sold in stores as currants are Zante currants, which actually are a small variety of raisin. If you can get real dried currants, these are a treat. Babas can also be made with dried plums, cherries, or any other dark dried fruit. **MAKES 12 CAKES.**

Dough

1	cup currants
½	cup dark rum
2	packages active dry yeast
½	cup warm water
2	tablespoons sugar
2	cups all-purpose flour
1	teaspoon salt
4	large eggs, beaten
½	cup unsalted butter, softened
¼	teaspoon grated orange zest

Rum syrup

2	cups water
1	cup sugar
1	cup dark rum

Soak currants in rum. In a large bowl combine yeast and sugar in warm water, and let stand until foamy, about 5 minutes. Add flour, and mix well. Gradually, add salt, eggs, butter, currant mixture, and orange zest, mixing well. Add another ¼ cup flour if needed. Cover bowl, and let rest for 15 minutes.

Turn out onto a lightly floured surface. Pull off golf-ball-sized pieces, and shape into balls. Place in buttered muffin cups. Cover with a cloth, and let rise until doubled, about 45 minutes.

Preheat oven to 375° F.

Bake for 25 minutes or until golden. Turn out of cups, and cool on a wire rack.

When babas have cooled, make rum syrup by bringing water and sugar quickly to a boil in a heavy pan. Reduce heat, and add rum. While syrup is hot, submerge babas, gently squeezing with tongs to fully absorb syrup. Set soaked babas aside to drain while dipping the rest. Place in layers at the bottom of a glass jar or a vase until near the top. Pour remaining syrup over babas, and cover with plastic wrap. Wait two weeks. Do not refrigerate. Serve with fresh whipped cream and fruit.

LORENZO'S RECOMMENDED READING

• Carol Field, *The Italian Baker* (New York: Harper-Collins 1985). This classic is where I started, and I have my nose in it for reference quite often.

• Harold McGee, *On Food and Cooking: The Science and Lore of the Kitchen*, rev. ed. (New York: Scribner, 2004). McGee writes more about the science and history than the actual preparation of food. This is real brain food.

• I recommend any cookbook by Giuliano Bugialli. This former language instructor from Florence brings his Italian cuisine to life vividly. I tend to appreciate cookbooks with more story than recipe these days. There are endless variations on bread formulas and cookie recipes, but I learn as much or more from the stories and the history surrounding the family recipe.

Kim Ode

FOLLOWING THE RHYTHMS OF LIFE

Var sa god!

GRANDMA ODE, CALLING US TO THE TABLE WITH HER HEARTY NORWEGIAN, "HELP YOURSELF!"

The recipes for the breads I like to bake are like almost everyone else's—some are family favorites whose origins are long lost to a recipe card written in longhand, others are adaptations of masterly recipes, and a few have come out of my head as I've grown more confident and curious about the whole process.

Most of my baking takes place in the wood-fired brick bread oven I built in our backyard, where temperatures flirt with 600° F. But the bread rarely burns. (Rarely.) It's a different kind of heat, the cool dough creating its own convection currents when it hits the hot bricks. And as each load of bread is completed and removed, the temperature drops, so I plan my schedule of baking to begin with, say, baguettes that need a quick flash of intense heat, moving through sourdough *boules* and *ciabatta,* and ending up with chocolate bread, whose sugar content requires a more moderate temperature.

At the end of the day, my husband builds a quick, hot fire to recharge the oven floor; then pushes it to the back, and we'll do some pizzas. As the oven continues to moderate, in goes a Dutch oven filled with a roast and vegetables to braise overnight. By the next day the oven is the right temperature for baking some granola and, eventually, for a few pans of Lorenzo's *grissini,* which need a slow, low bake.

I love this rhythm.

But I also bake in my "domestic" oven and have adapted these recipes for use in any kitchen.

Ihla's Oatmeal Bread

My mother, Ihla, once took first place in a baking competition sponsored by the South Dakota Farm Bureau for her oatmeal bread. Typically, she gave the credit to the recipe. I thought it was unbelievably impressive that my mom had won a prize for her bread, at the same time thinking, "Well, duh." It was that good. **MAKES 2 LOAVES.**

2 cups boiling water
1 cup quick-cooking oatmeal
4 tablespoons shortening
½ cup light molasses
½ cup brown sugar, packed
2 teaspoons salt
1 package active dry yeast
½ cup warm water
5½ cups all-purpose flour

In a large bowl pour boiling water over oatmeal. Stir in shortening, molasses, brown sugar, and salt. Cool to lukewarm. In a small bowl dissolve yeast in warm water, and let sit until foamy, about 5 minutes. Add to oatmeal mixture. Stir in enough flour so that dough comes together in a ball and can be handled. (It will be sticky.) Gradually, knead in remaining flour. Place dough in an oiled bowl, turning to coat top, cover with plastic wrap, and let rise until doubled.

Turn out onto a lightly floured surface, and divide in half. Shape each piece into a loaf, and place in a greased loaf pan. Cover with a cloth, and let rise until doubled. Gently brush with milk, and sprinkle with additional oats.

Preheat oven to 350° F.

Bake for 45 minutes or until loaves sound hollow when tapped. Remove from pans, and cool on a wire rack.

Grandma Ode's Norwegian Flatbread

Grandma would always make a huge batch for Thanksgiving, and we'd keep eating it well into the winter. While it's possible to do alone, this is a companionable process with one person rolling while another watches each flatbread in the oven. Flatbread will stay tasty for weeks stored in a box lined with wax paper. We always saved the box in which the most recent pair of Red Wing work boots came, but I've since found that any box works just as well—only with less flair. **MAKES A LOT.**

- ½ cup shortening
- ½ cup sugar
- ¾ cup white corn syrup
- 2 teaspoons salt
- 1 cup graham flour
- 1 cup cornmeal
- 1 teaspoon baking soda
- 2 cups buttermilk
- 3 to 3½ cups all-purpose flour

Preheat oven to 375° F.

With a mixer, cream together sugar, shortening, and corn syrup; add salt. In another bowl stir together graham flour, cornmeal, and baking soda. Add to creamed mixture in three batches, alternating with buttermilk. Add just enough white flour to make a stiff dough.

Take a ball of dough about the size of a golf ball, and roll as thin as possible on a lightly floured pastry cloth. A special grooved flatbread rolling pin works best, but this can be done with a regular rolling pin and a firm touch.

Lift onto an ungreased baking sheet, and gently score with a pastry wheel or pizza cutter into serving-size pieces. Bake until edges begin to brown, about 5 minutes. Keep an eye on it. By the time you're done rolling the next flatbread, it's time to check on the one in the oven. Cool on a wire rack. Break apart on scored lines.

Summit Beer Brown-again Bread

Beer adds a subtle tenderness and flavor to breads. St. Paul's Summit Brewery makes a fine Great Northern Porter, and its deep brown color made me think of other brown ingredients such as browned butter, barley malt syrup, and coffee. For texture I added some millet, an ancient seed that's gaining popularity as a source of protein, fiber, and other nutrients. Millet has been around since the Stone Age, cultivated from China to Africa to Europe. Of course, the truth is that many of the world's grains have been around that long, which then makes eating bread practically instinctive—something we are born to do. **MAKES 2 LOAVES.**

¼	cup unsalted butter (½ stick), browned
¼	cup millet, toasted
12	ounces Summit Great Northern Porter, or similar dark beer
1	scant teaspoon instant coffee granules
¼	cup barley malt syrup
1	tablespoon active dry yeast
¼	cup cornmeal
1	cup whole wheat flour
3	to 4 cups bread flour
2	teaspoons salt

In a small saucepan melt butter over medium heat, watching carefully as it turns to a deep chestnut brown, but no darker. This only takes a minute. Pour into a small bowl to stop the cooking. Then in the same pan, without wiping it clean, toast millet over low heat until you hear a few popping sounds. Scrape into a small bowl, and set aside.

In the saucepan gently heat beer to lukewarm. Stir in instant coffee and barley malt syrup.

In a large bowl whisk together yeast, cornmeal, whole wheat flour, and 3 cups bread flour. Add beer mixture and browned butter, and stir until dough comes together and pulls away from sides of bowl, adding more flour if needed. Add salt and millet, and mix well.

Turn out onto a well-floured surface, and let sit for 15 minutes under an inverted bowl. This resting period gives the flour time to fully absorb the liquid, which helps the dough firm up, making it easier to knead. Knead until smooth and elastic. Place in an oiled bowl, turning to coat top, cover with plastic wrap, and let rise until doubled, about 1 hour.

Turn out onto a lightly floured surface, and divide in half. Shape into a round *boule* or a loaf shape, and place on a baking sheet sprinkled with cornmeal. Sprinkle tops with flour. Cover with a cloth, and let rise until doubled, about 1 hour.

Preheat oven to 400° F.

With a box cutter or sharp knife, make several slashes across tops of loaves. Bake for 30 to 35 minutes or until a loaf sounds hollow when tapped on bottom or an instant-read thermometer reads 200° F. Cool on a rack.

Fig and Lemon Sourdough with Thyme

Klecko calls this my signature loaf, and it won a sweepstakes award at the bread club's 2005 baking contest. But anyone comparing that one to this might accuse me of forgery, because I've kept tweaking the recipe. Its original inspiration is from Nancy Silverton's Breads of the La Brea Bakery, *but I've added lemon zest, thyme, and a purée of Calimyrna figs. The final variation was using a brick starter instead of my liquid "Glinda"; a bread with such dense ingredients needed a more supportive dough. I think this one's a keeper. It's lovely sliced thin, plain, or toasted. Try it with a smear of blue cheese.* **MAKES 3 LOAVES.**

- ½ cup dried Calimyrna figs, coarsely chopped
- ½ cup hot water
- 1 tablespoon active dry yeast
- ½ cup warm water
- 1 cup brick starter (see recipe on page 40)
- 3 tablespoons sugar
- 3 cups bread flour

1½ teaspoons salt
 2 tablespoons cornmeal
    Grated rind of 1 lemon
 ½ teaspoon dried thyme or 1 teaspoon fresh thyme
 1 cup black mission figs, stems removed, cut in halves or thirds
 1 egg, beaten with 1 teaspoon water

Combine Calimyrna figs and hot water in blender, and process to a purée. Set aside. Dissolve yeast in warm water, and let sit until foamy, about 5 minutes. In a large bowl combine brick starter with fig purée. Add yeast and sugar. Gradually, add flour, salt, and cornmeal, and mix well. Add lemon and thyme, and mix well. Add black mission figs, mixing just until incorporated.

KIM'S BAKING TIPS

• I prefer using rapid-rise yeast, also sold as instant or bread machine yeast. This is a finer-grained yeast than the regular stuff, so I can whisk it directly into the flour without first dissolving it in water. I've not found that it makes the bread rise any faster, but it stream-lines the mixing process. You can use the two interchangeably in recipes.

• My favorite tool is my bench knife. With it you can scoop up chopped ingredients, cut dough into pieces, manipulate a soft dough until it's workable, and scrape clean a shaggy, floury counter.

• A box cutter with replaceable single-edge razor blades is great for scoring the tops of loaves.

• Scoring releases steam but also allows you to affect how the bread "blooms" in the oven. Some-times, a cut straight down into the loaf serves the purpose, such as the X in Irish soda bread. But to get that artisanal ridge or "ear" that stands up from the loaf, hold the blade at a slight angle and slit just beneath the dough's surface, about a half inch into the loaf. To keep this motion from becoming a gash, it helps to say the word "slit" as you're making the slice. Really.

• When I'm forming the loaves, I try to use little or no flour on my countertop so that there's more friction to help make a taut, firm shape.

• Don't rush. My worst baking days are when I feel pressured by time and start trying to hurry along the process.

• But I do like to sketch out a bread schedule the night before; it helps me organize the day so that I know whether I can drive my daughter over to a friend's house between the first and the second rise.

Turn out onto a lightly floured surface, and knead until dough is smooth and figs are well distributed, about 5 minutes. Place in an oiled bowl, turning to coat top, cover with plastic wrap, and let rise until doubled, about 1 hour.

Divide into 4 pieces and shape each into a round *boule*. Place on a baking sheet lined with parchment paper. Cover with a cloth, and let rise until doubled, about 1 hour.

Preheat oven to 400° F.

Brush loaves with egg glaze, cut several slits in top of each, and bake for 20 minutes. Check *boules,* and rotate if necessary. Their high sugar content may cause them to brown unevenly. Bake for another 20 minutes until loaf sounds hollow when tapped or an instant-read thermometer reads 190° F. Cool on a rack.

Sour-squared Bread

Like the infamous chocolate cake with the secret ingredient, the sauerkraut in this sourdough melts almost into nothingness as it bakes but creates a moist, tangy bread that's perfect for sandwiches. Don't fear the amount of yeast called for; you need it to counteract the effects of the sauerkraut juice.

MAKES 2 LOAVES.

2	tablespoons active dry yeast
½	cup warm water
1	cup brick starter (see recipe on page 40)
2	cups sauerkraut, with juice
6	cups bread flour
2½	tablespoons salt
2	tablespoons caraway seeds, if desired

Dissolve yeast in warm water, and set aside until foamy, about 5 minutes. Stir yeast mixture into starter to loosen it somewhat, and then mix in sauerkraut and juice. Begin adding flour 1 cup at a time until dough comes together in a stiff ball. Add salt, and continue mixing. Add caraway seeds.

Turn out onto a lightly floured surface, and knead until smooth and elastic, about 10 minutes. Place in an oiled bowl, turning to coat top, cover with plastic wrap, and let rise until doubled, about 1 hour.

Divide into 2 pieces, and shape into round *boules*. Place on a baking sheet lined with parchment. With a razor blade make several slits across top. Cover with a cloth, and let rise until doubled, about 1 hour. You can also shape and place dough in greased loaf pans.

Preheat oven to 400° F.

Bake 40 to 50 minutes or until loaf sounds hollow when tapped on bottom.

Jackie's Carrot Baguettes

My friend Jackie Zimmerman also loves to bake bread and shared this recipe that she translated from her native Swiss. It's a crusty, savory loaf with a warm orange color that provides a wonderful contrast in a basket of mixed breads. Try it toasted with cream cheese. **MAKES 2 LOAVES.**

¾	cup whole wheat flour
3	cups bread flour
1	package active dry yeast
2	teaspoons barley malt syrup
½	cup buttermilk, room temperature
¼	teaspoon ground cardamom
2	cups finely grated carrots (about 3 medium carrots)
⅔	cup carrot juice
1½	teaspoons salt

In a large bowl mix together flours, then make a depression in center. In a small bowl mix together yeast, malt syrup, and buttermilk. Pour into depression, and let stand until foamy, about 5 minutes. Add cardamom, grated carrots, carrot juice, and salt, and begin stirring liquid, gradually pulling in flour from sides until a soft dough forms and pulls away clean from sides.

Turn out onto a lightly floured surface, and knead, adding more flour if necessary, until dough is smooth and elastic. Place in an oiled bowl, turning to coat top, cover with plastic wrap, and let rise until doubled, about 1 hour.

Turn out onto a lightly floured surface, and divide in half. Form 2 long baguettes, and place on a baking sheet lined with parchment paper or dusted with cornmeal. Cover with a cloth, and let rise until doubled, about 30 minutes.

Preheat oven to 425° F, and move racks to lowest and middle positions.

With a sharp knife or razor blade, make angled slashes across tops of loaves. Place a pan on lower shelf, and then place loaves on middle shelf. Carefully, pour some boiling water into pan, and quickly close oven door. Bake for 10 minutes. Then remove pan of water from oven, reduce heat to 350° F, and bake for 30 to 35 minutes. Loaves should sound hollow when tapped on bottom. Cool on a wire rack.

Bittersweet Chocolate–Ginger Bread

I love a not-too-sweet chocolate bread, and it's my daughter's favorite— as long as it's plain chocolate. I persist in wanting, however, to add various embellishments, such as dried cherries or cut-up apricots, both of which veer toward the sweet. But the addition of candied ginger proved the solution to jazzing up the bread, while tempering the sweet with some heat. It's a sophisticated combination. **MAKES 2 LOAVES.**

1 package active dry yeast
⅓ cup warm water
4½ cups bread flour
½ cup sugar
⅓ cup unsweetened high-quality dark cocoa powder
2 teaspoons salt
1¼ cups warm water
4 ounces high-quality bittersweet chocolate, chopped in ½-inch pieces
½ cup candied ginger, finely chopped
1 egg, beaten with 1 teaspoon water

Dissolve yeast in warm water, and set aside until foamy, about 5 minutes. In a medium bowl mix flour, sugar, cocoa, and salt. Stir remaining 1¼ cups water into dissolved yeast, and then stir into flour mixture. Turn out onto a lightly floured surface, and knead until smooth and elastic, 8 to 10 minutes. Knead in chocolate and ginger. Place dough in an oiled bowl, turning to coat top, cover with plastic wrap, and let rise until doubled, about 1 hour.

Turn out onto a lightly floured surface, and divide in half. Form each half into desired shape, round *boules* or oval loaves, and place on a baking sheet covered with parchment paper. Cover with a cloth, and let rise until doubled, about 1 hour.

Preheat oven to 450° F.

Brush loaves with egg wash, and then make a few decorative slashes across tops. Bake for 10 minutes. Then reduce heat to 350° F, and bake for 30 minutes or until bread sounds hollow when tapped on bottom. Cool on wire racks.

Gluten-free Rice Loaf

It's a blithe life I live, able to tolerate all manner of wheat. But as I ran into more people whose bodies rebelled at wheat, I wondered what gluten-free baking was all about. It's a challenging problem and one that bakers across the country are tackling. From my limited experience the loaves are denser and moister than typical bread—nothing that you'd build a ham sandwich with. Cobbled together from several recipes from different sources, here's a bread that one gluten-intolerant friend said is excellent toasted, which was all she really wanted, something on which she could spread her friend's homemade jam. This recipe is adapted from one on the Red Star Yeast website. Xanthan gum is available in most grocery stores. **MAKES 1 LOAF.**

> 2½ cups brown rice flour
> ½ cup soy flour
> ½ cup potato starch flour or cornstarch
> 2½ teaspoons xanthan gum

1½ teaspoons salt

½ cup nonfat dry milk

2 packages active dry yeast

3 large eggs, lightly beaten

1 teaspoon cider vinegar

3 tablespoons canola oil

1½ cups water

Turn on oven to 225° F for 2 minutes. Turn off.

In a medium bowl whisk together dry ingredients. In a small bowl whisk together wet ingredients. Add wet ingredients to dry, stirring just until the consistency of cake batter. Don't overmix. Scrape into a well-greased loaf pan.

Place in warm oven for 10 minutes. Remove from oven, cover with a cloth, and let rise until dough reaches edge of pan, about 1 hour.

Preheat oven to 325° F.

Gently place pan in oven. (Because the dough lacks gluten, it's more fragile.) Bake for 1 hour or until a wooden pick inserted in middle of loaf comes out clean. Turn out of pan, and let cool on a wire rack.

Bialy Cracker Bread

A bialy *is an eastern European bread, kind of like a bagel but topped with a distinctive "schmear" of onion and poppy seeds. This cracker bread is a flatter variation on that theme.*

Dough

1 package active dry yeast

1⅓ cup warm water

1 tablespoon extra-virgin olive oil

1½ tablespoons honey

3½ cups all-purpose flour

1 teaspoon salt

Topping

 2 medium yellow onions, in ½-inch dice
 2 tablespoons olive oil
 5 green onions, sliced thin and well into the green
 2 tablespoons poppy seeds
   Coarse salt such as *fleur de sel*
 1 egg white, beaten with 1 teaspoon water

Preheat oven to 450° F.

Dissolve yeast in warm water, and let stand until foamy, about 5 minutes. Add oil, honey, 3 cups flour, and salt, and mix until a firm dough forms. Turn out onto a lightly floured counter, and knead, adding additional flour as necessary. Place in an oiled bowl, turning to coat top, cover with plastic wrap, and let rise, about 45 minutes.

Sauté yellow onions in olive oil over medium heat until translucent, about 10 minutes. Remove from heat, and stir in poppy seeds and green onions. In a small bowl whisk egg white with water.

Turn dough out onto a dry surface, and divide in half. Place each half on an oiled baking sheet, and pat into a rectangle that covers about half the surface. Cover with a cloth, and let rest for 10 minutes. Keep patting dough toward edges (it will stretch more easily now) until as thin as possible. You'll cover almost the whole surface.

Brush each half with egg white mixture, and then spread onion and poppy seed mixture evenly over each. Lightly sprinkle with coarse salt or *fleur de sel* and several grindings of black pepper. With a pastry wheel or pizza cutter, lightly score dough into desired size of pieces.

Bake about 10 to 15 minutes, switching pans halfway through to ensure even baking. Cool on wire racks, and break along scored lines to serve.

Breakfast Scones

Scone is one of those "tomato-tomahto" words. Half the people say it to rhyme with "stone" and the other half have been corrected often enough to have given in and say it to rhyme with "gone." Which makes sense since gone is what these will be at any breakfast table within minutes of sitting down. These are delicate scones, the high proportion of butter and shortening to flour and oats making them very "short" and crumbly, and thus rich and delicious. Funny how that works. They come together in about five minutes and bake in fifteen, so they're perfect for satisfying a burst of early morning inspiration. Substitute any dried fruit you like. **MAKES 8 SCONES.**

1 ¼	cups all-purpose flour
1	teaspoon baking powder
½	teaspoon baking soda
¼	teaspoon salt
¼	cup dark brown sugar, packed
4	tablespoons unsalted butter
¼	cup vegetable shortening
1	cup old-fashioned oatmeal
⅔	cup dried plums, snipped into small pieces
⅓	cup buttermilk

Preheat oven to 375° F.

In a medium bowl mix flour, baking powder, soda, salt, and brown sugar. With a pastry cutter or two knives, cut in butter and shortening until well distributed in small pieces. Stir in oatmeal and dried plums. Add buttermilk, mixing just until moistened. Knead inside bowl for 5 or 6 turns, place on ungreased baking sheet, and then pat into a 7-inch circle. Cut into 8 wedges, and then gently move them slightly apart, leaving about 1 inch between each wedge.

Bake for 15 minutes and serve warm.

HOW TO START YOUR OWN BREAD CLUB

BY KLECKO

When I first launched the bread club concept, I felt pretty confident that the project would be successful. For more than two decades, I'd specialized in creating breadlines for an entire city. How hard could it be to teach a handful of home bakers how to make a decent loaf?

The first year I did a lot of talking. Every session had demonstrations that incorporated science, theory, and bakers' math. As the group's self-assurance began to increase, so did their conversations. But to my surprise, folks weren't discussing improper pumpernickel percentages or debating fermentation times.

Instead, their topics were more romantic in nature.

When I passed by a group making *ciabatta* at one station, I overheard several women reminiscing about a baker from the Iron Range who gave their mothers some cake yeast. Over by the Hobart mixer, a prized baking pupil was comparing the caraway dough in the mixing bowl to the breads of New York that she treasured in her youth.

At that moment I began to realize that the majority of my baking companions were on individual quests to re-create particular breads and that those breads would serve almost as passports to a cherished family member or a significant place.

So before I share the prototype of our club, I want to remind you that having a plan is good but giving the club permission to evolve is even better. The website for the St. Paul Bread Club can be found at http://spbc.info.

Here are some helpful hints for forming your own bread club:

Develop a timeline. Before I even opened the doors to the bakery, I drew up a loose itinerary of how I thought the first year should go. When it became time to choose how often the club should meet, the general consensus was that quarterly gatherings would be enough to keep a core group rooted without overwhelming or creating too much work for any of the participants.

Avoid obstacles. Whenever anything of value is created, exploitation will ride its coattails. That's why it's so critical that no money should be involved. Any time membership fees are assessed or budgets are created, differences in opinion are almost certain to cause division. Why risk it?

Create a space. It isn't necessary to hold bread club meetings in a bakery. Our first year was spent in the conference room of a local food co-op. But if your heart is set on actually having access to baking equipment, you might want to consider contacting several churches. Most are equipped with commercial equipment that doesn't get used a lot.

Celebrate baking. An annual competition serves several purposes. For the members a bake-off is an opportunity to exhibit the skills they have worked on throughout the year. For the club the contest is an ideal way to involve family, friends, and media.

Final thoughts. My baking masters used to tell me, "It's more honorable to train a winner than to be a winner." It is never admirable to hoard instruction, recipes, and, most of all, encouragement. If you keep this in mind, you're destined to bake well.

A FEW OF OUR
FAVORITE THINGS

Bread is the culinary equivalent of a theater understudy. It hovers in the background of many meals, always dependable, but rarely called upon to star. It provides a sense of security, a peace of mind that people needn't ever leave the table hungry. And when something does go wrong at mealtime—whether the roast burned or hockey practice ran late—bread can always be called to center stage, slathered with mayonnaise and ham, or peanut butter and jelly.

Still, most people generally don't spend a lot of time thinking about bread. So it's inspiring to hear what these home bakers have to say about their explorations into flavors, textures, and other embellishments.

Marie Wang is always on the lookout for what she calls "big flavors" for her breads. Ginger is one of her favorite spices, a natural since it infuses the Chinese cooking she was raised on, but it's also a staple of the Thanksgiving and Christmas baking that she enjoys.

She also likes the flavor that fat brings to a recipe. "Butter by a long shot," she said. "I love the flavor of butter and the way it makes other foods shine."

Foster Cole has become a seeker—and disciple—of honey. As it takes on the subtle flavor variations of whatever nectar its bees imbibed, so it provides nuances to a bread. "There are more varieties of honey than you'd imagine," said Foster, who recommends a trip through the Minnesota Honey Producer's bee and honey pavilion at the State Fair. You can sample honeys with hints of basswood, clover, thistle, and goldenrod.

Bill Middeke is a great proponent of honey, as well, but also likes substituting different beers for his liquids in a bread. For him bread is a willing vehicle for strong flavors. Caraway is not to everyone's liking; he loves it. Likewise, his sweet rolls aren't shy with the cinnamon.

Will Powers urges bakers to explore their spice cabinets. "Grind some cumin with kosher salt and peppercorns and sprinkle this on a flatbread," he said. "Then try something else next week."

Will also experiments with different oils. The roasted sesame oil in his midnight bulgur bread is a prime example of a secret ingredient since it's not really the sesame that you taste but something . . . deeper. Markets carry more varieties of oils these days, whether made from almond or walnuts or flaxseed, so the possibilities are intriguing.

Lorenzo tends to seek out combinations of ingredients. One of his favorite combos is cracked pepper and almonds, perhaps baked in a bread made with his favorite semolina flour and then topped with one of the sea salts that he collects for their varying flavors and colors.

Ingredients are only as limited as your imagination.

I still remember the time Klecko called me at work to have me guess what was in the Victorian loaves he'd just made for Valentine's Day. Bakers of that era, by the nature of the job, used to work all night to have bread ready for their morning customers. So they didn't see much of their wives.

Wisely, they made a special, flower-filled loaf for their sweethearts on Valentine's Day. In tribute to them, Klecko made a dough into which he kneaded edible pansies and sunflower petals, so each slice was a bouquet of multicolored flecks. Once baked, he further embellished the loaves with chocolate.

So think outside the cookbook. Then go for it.

CONTRIBUTORS

David S. Cargo is a computer programmer who lives with his wife in the Highland Park neighborhood of St. Paul. When he's not baking and developing new recipes, he's maintaining the St. Paul Bread Club contact list and website. When he can find the time, he also enjoys gardening and pinhole photography.

Elaine and Foster Cole bake and garden in New Brighton. They enjoy traveling through the prairies, back roads, and small towns of the Midwest, among other places.

Char Johnson and her husband, Rollie, now live in Vadnais Heights and have five grown children and ten grandchildren. When not baking, Char enjoys knitting, craft painting, walking, water aerobics, and spoiling grandkids.

When **Dan "Klecko" McGleno** is not baking bread you'll likely find him coaching Little League baseball, staring at a chess board, or playing in a field with his Jack Russell terriers.

Lauren "Lorenzo" Allen is a bread baker and instructor in St. Paul and a member of the Bread Bakers Guild of America. He often can be seen biking up and down the paths near the Mississippi River. He and his wife are both avid readers and lovers of live music.

Bill Middeke and his wife of thirty-five years live with one daughter and a miniature dachshund in Eden Prairie. In the warmer weather, he morphs into his alter ego of Bicycle Bill to raise funds for HIV/AIDS–related charities in what has become his annual Red Ribbon Ride.

Ron Miller is a Realtor and tinkerer who likes to spend time in his workshop. He fixes things around his house and other places, although he doesn't feel as adept as he used to when climbing ladders. He also enjoys working in his garden and spending time with family, especially his grandson.

Kim Ode is a staff writer at the *Star Tribune* and lives in Edina with her husband and two teenagers. When she's not baking, she enjoys gardening, sailing, volleyball, and playing trombone in the Calhoun Isles Community Band.

Will Powers bakes bread for his wife, Cheryl Miller (and for pals and relatives, too), in their home across the street from White Bear Lake. He also oversees the design and production of books at the Minnesota Historical Society Press and teaches typography at the College of Visual Arts in St. Paul.

Pat Roberts lives in Rosemount with her husband; her son and daughter have married and live nearby with their families. When Pat isn't baking to share with friends, neighbors, and coworkers, she is creating hand-stamped cards for them or teaching her three preschool-aged granddaughters how to do both. She also enjoys gardening and will share her plants as freely as her baking and cards.

Mark Shafer is retired after working forty years at the Buckbee Mears Company making fine machined goods. He is a woodworker and a cabinetmaker, an amateur guitar player, and an old car buff who owns a 1951 Plymouth Cambridge.

Carol Sturgeleski lives with her husband, Bernie. Together they have raised six children. When she's not baking, she loves to garden, sew on her computerized sewing machine, and sing in the choir at church.

Karen Vogl has her own business and works out of her home, which often allows time for baking bread during the day. In addition to baking, she enjoys biking, hiking, cross-country skiing, and sewing for her grandchildren.

Marie Wang bemoans that there truly is only so much bread that one can stuff into oneself. She occupies her remaining time primarily with toddler-chasing (and is thankful she has only one at this point), making exotic foods, and her part-time psychiatry practice.

Susan Steger Welsh is a St. Paul poet and writer whose first poetry collection, *Rafting on the Water Table* (New Rivers Press, 2000), was a finalist for a Minnesota Book Award. She writes, bakes, gardens, and feeds people in the almost hundred-year-old house where she and her husband have raised two members of the next generation of bread bakers.

Members of the St. Paul Bread Club whose recipes are included in this book. Front row, from left: Lorenzo Allen, Pat Roberts, Foster Cole; second row, from left: Char Johnson, Kim Ode, Marie Wang, Will Powers, Mark Shafer, Ron Miller, David Cargo; back row: Karen Vogl, Klecko, Bill Middeke. Not pictured: Elaine Cole, Carol Sturgeleski, and Susan Steger Welsh.

INDEX

Page numbers in **bold** indicate definitions.

Recipes

PERMISSIONS

The recipe Pane di Como is from *The Italian Baker* by Carol Field © 1985. Reprinted by permission of HarperCollins Publishers.

The recipe Baked Puffed Flatbread is reprinted with permission from the January/February 1999 issue of *Cook's Illustrated* magazine. For a trial issue of *Cook's Illustrated* call 1-800-526-8442. Selected articles and recipes, as well as subscription information, are available online at www.cooksillustrated.com.

The recipes Cheddar Cheese Bread, Sugarplum Bread, and Buttermilk Whole Wheat Bread are from *The Complete Book of Breads* by Bernard Clayton © 1973. Reprinted by permission of Simon & Schuster Publishers.

The recipe Hearty Whole Grain Bread is adapted from a recipe from *The Chicago Tribune Cookbook: Contemporary and Classic Favorites*, edited by Jeanmarie Brownson © 1989. Reprinted by permission of Chicago Review Press.